PA-KUA

YELLOW EMPEROR

LAO TZU

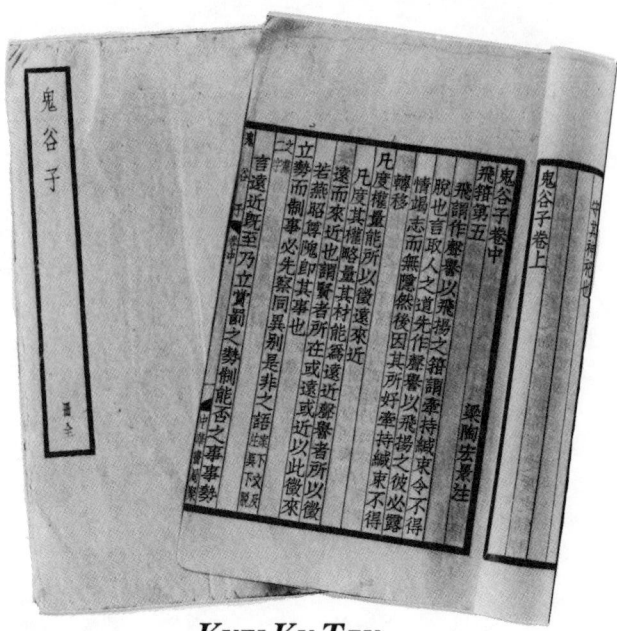

KUEI KU TZU
SAGE KUEI KU'S BOOK

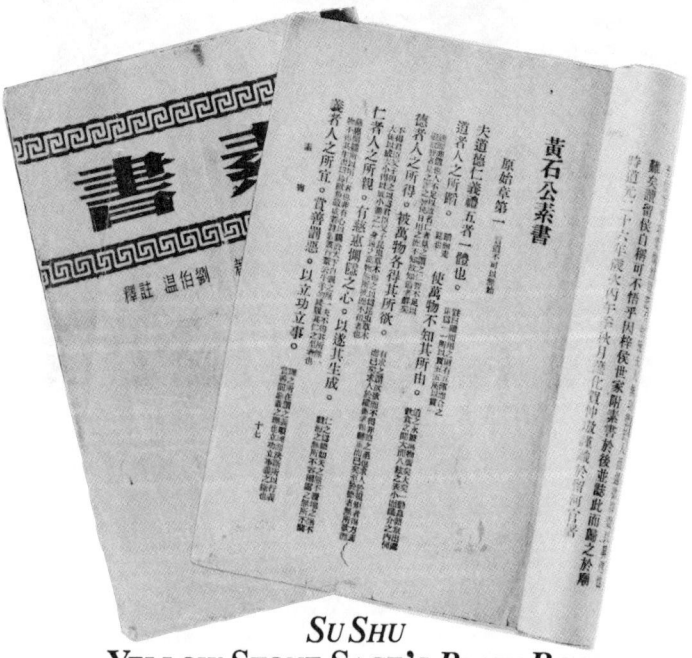

SU SHU
YELLOW STONE SAGE'S *PLAIN BOOK*

THE INTEGRAL MANAGEMENT OF TAO

Complete Achievement

DR. STEPHEN T. CHANG

TAO PUBLISHING

Copyright © 1988, 1991 by Stephen T. Chang

Published by Tao Publishing
2' ~~Tao Longevity LLC
   P.O. Box 33910
S Reno, NV 89533~~ 4132

All rights reserved. No part of this book may be reproduced, stored in a retrieval system, or transmitted, in any form or by any means, electronic, mechanical, photocopying, recording, or otherwise, without permission in writing from the publisher.

First printing, 1988
Second printing, 1991
Third printing, 1994

Printed in the United States of America

Library of Congress Cataloging in Publication Data

Chang, Stephen Thomas, Date
    The integral management of Tao: complete achievement/by Stephen T. Chang.
       p. cm.
    Includes index.
    ISBN 0-942196-08-2
    1. Management—China—History. 2. Taoism. I. Title.
HD70.C5C386 1986
658'.00951—dc19   88-20070
                                                               CIP

ABOUT THE AUTHOR

Dr. Stephen Thomas Chang is an internationally well-known scholar. His great grandfather was professor to Emperor Hsien Feng and the first Chinese ambassador to the United Kingdom. Trained in both law and medicine, Dr. Chang holds doctorates in philosophy and medicine. He has taught in business schools since 1961 and has lectured world-wide on various aspects of Taoism. He has headed several foreign and domestic corporations and is the author of the following books:

The Complete Book of Acupuncture,
The Great Tao,
The Tao of Sexology (The Best Way to Make Love Work),
The Complete System of Self-Healing: Internal Exercises,
The Tao of Balanced Diet: Secrets of a Thin and Healthy Body.

Several books are university and hospital textbooks and have been translated into ten languages. Dr. Chang is the founder and chairman of the Foundation of Tao.

ACKNOWLEDGEMENTS

The author gratefully acknowledges the support of:

Bart Body, Ph.D.
Gita Body, Ph.D.
Vera Brown
Luke Chang, Ph.D.
Shirley Dahn
Mako Hayamizu
Gita LaBrentz
Tony Lin, M.B.A.
Catherine Lindseth,
John Lindseth, Ph.D.
Sam Matthew
Fay Mongraw
Frank Mongraw
Fernando Moreno, M.B.A.
Bjorn Overbye, M.D.
Grace Roessler, Ph.D.
Cecilia Rosenfeld, M.D.
Phillip Schaeffer
Eugene Schwartz
Stephen Soja
Jim Sykes
Leonard Worthington, J.D.
Nancy Worthington
Diana Wu, Ph.D.
Thomas Yang

Contents

PREFACE 15
INTRODUCTION 17
    First Role Model: Chiang, Shang, The Great Duke ....
    The Tao of Management ....
        Nine Styles of Management ....
PART I: BASIC KNOWLEDGE
1. THE TAO OF EVOLUTION 33
    Five Kingdoms ....
    Seven Levels of Humankind ....
    Three Folds of the Body ....
    Seven Ages of Human History ....
2. THE TAO OF YIN AND YANG RELATIVISM ....
    Two Golden Ages ....
    Yin and Yang and Their Importance Defined ....
    Six Types of Yin-Yang Interaction ....
    Six Laws: Operation of the Universe ....
    Second Role Model: Su, Chin, the Greatest CEO,
        and Sage Kuei Ku ....
3. THE TAO OF EIGHT ATTITUDES 61
    Becoming the Right Person ....
    Accomplishing Missions ....
    Yin-Yang in an Algebraic Formula ....
    Eight Trigrams, Reservoirs of Knowledge ....
    Attitude of Heaven (Goals) ....
    Attitude of Water (Discipline)...
    Attitude of Mountain (Tolerance) ....
    Attitude of Thunder (Creativeness) ....
    Attitude of Wind (Loyalty) ....
    Attitude of Fire (Giving) ....

Contents

Attitude of Earth (Retirement) ....
Attitude of Lake (Entertainment) ....
Systemization by Japanese Corporations and Their
    Competitive Power ....
Eight Blessings ....
Eight Exercises (for self-improvement and insurance) ....

4. THE TAO OF POSITIONING 85
Five Groups of Possible Factors Leading to the
    Obtainment of Positions ....
Six Strategies to Guarantee a Position ....
Six Situations That Jeopardize a Position ....
Four Ways of Safeguarding a Position ....
Third Role Model: Moses ....

5. THE TAO OF FIVE-STAR SYSTEM 93
Two Hemispheres of the Brain ....
Five-Element Theory ....
Personality Type: Water ....
Personality Type: Metal ....
Personality Type: Fire ....
Personality Type: Wood ....
Personality Type: Earth ....
Personality-to-Job Matching for Highest Productivity ....
Five-Element Departments in an Organization ....
Diagnostic Instrument for Organizations ....
Ancient Taoist Structure ....

6. THE TAO OF PSYCHO-DYNAMICS ....
Human Nature and Styles of Management ....
Psycho-Dynamics (truth of human nature) ....
Centripetal Perception ....
Centrifugal Perception ....
Rules of Physics Dominating Human Psychology ....
Analytic Geometric Forms ....
Principle of Loss (executives cannot survive without it) ....

CONTENTS

PART II: LOFTY PERFORMANCE
7. THE TAO OF LEADERSHIP 129
   Performance of Commander Chang ....
   Fourth Role Model: Marquis Chang, Liang and
      Sage Yellow Stone ....
   Qualities of a Leader ....
   Leader's Responsibilities to His Followers ....
   Leader's Impression on Followers ....
   Decision Making ....
   The Power of the Leader (skills to ensure a leader's
      performance) ....
      Persuasion ....
      Reward ....
      Being with Followers ....
      Budget ....
   Organization ....
   Sacrifices of the Leader ....
      Loneliness ....
      Freedom ....
      Security ....
   Counteraction (of leadership) ....
      Scheme of Pretense ....
      Scheme of Jurisdiction ....
      Swindling Scheme ....
   Grades of Leadership ....
      Leadership of Hate ....
      Leadership of Fear ....
      Leadership of Happiness ....
      Leadership of Invisibility ....
      Emperor Yao ....
8. THE TAO OF COMPLETE RESOLUTION
   Three Mental Functions 159
   Classes of Decisions ....

Contents

 According to Law ....
 According to Custom ....
 According to Intuition ....
 According to Inference ....
 According to Rational Confirmation ....
Information ....
 Types of Information (ten basics everyone ought to know)
 Sources of Information (five different sources for
  collecting information according to Sun Tzu) ....
Thinking Process (that ensures capability) ....
 Suspicion ....
 Supposition ....
 Analysis ....
  Five Relations (unparalleled method for helping
   you think) ....
  Functions of Five Relations ....
  Fifteen Samenesses ....
Composition (Taoist method to ensure greatest perfection) ....
Final Decision ....
 Three Reasons for the Occurrence of Wrong Decisions ....
 Styles of Decision Making ....
  Decision Making by a Group ....
  Decision Making by a Leader ....
  Decision Making by a Brain Trust ....
 Fifth Role Model: Marquis Chu-Ko, Liang ....
 Decision-Making Results (that are foreseeable) ....
 Optimizing Results ....
  Internal Exercises to Balance the Thinking Process ....
9. THE TAO OF INTERCOMMUNICATION 187
 Messages ....
  Internal Message Chaos ....
  Intercourse Chaos ....
   Illness ....

Contents

- Fear
- Worry
- Anger
- Joy
- Fifth Role Model: Jesus
- Interpretation
  - Buddhist Monk (story)
  - Four Procedures of Interpretation
    - Essence of Movement
    - Picturing
    - Evidence
    - Unmistaken Conclusion
    - Mr. B.'s Case
- Persuasion
  - Orders (how to make others truly listen)
    - Three Rules of Order Giving
    - Two Forbiddens
  - Ordinary Persuasion (negotiate everything and make specific or non-specific people truly listen)
    - Impressiveness and Test to Increase Persuasive Power
    - Confidence (establishing)
    - Reflex
    - Classification of People
      - Personality
      - Background
      - Dislikes
    - Principles of Advantage and Disadvantage
      - Hsiang-Pi
      - Persuasive Skills
      - Testimonial
    - Presentation
      - Inductive Logic

Contents

    Deductive Logic
    Taoist Quaternary Logic (for indisputable presentations)
    More Testimonials
    Further Techniques
    Suggestion (effective presentation to and implementation of ideas for superiors)
    Yin-Yang Pairs for Effective Conduct (subordinate speaking skills)
    Effective Conduct before the Superior
    Yen, Yin, the Famous Diplomat
10. THE TAO OF RICHES AND FAME 225
    Weight Watching (organizational health-care)
    Smallness (secret of true success)
    Greed (evaluation of money, power, and fame)
    Rules for Money Lovers
    Monetary Rules
    New Age of Management
    Mission First, Profit Second (for true and everlasting reward)
    Saving the Company, Saving the World
CONCLUSION 233
    Blueprint (precious gift to readers)
    Sixth Role Model: Kung-Sun, Yang, Lord of Fifteen Cities
APPENDIX 245
    Eye Exercises
    Stomach Rubbing Exercise
    Tao of Balanced Diet
    Morning and Evening Prayers
INDEX 263

PREFACE

As long as human beings exist, management will exist. As long as two people must live together, management will be needed. Although the instruments that enable human beings to perform may change in time, the principles of human psychology and behavior never change. The best management has always been the key that unlocks human potential. Therefore, from the household to the White House, good management is a common necessity.

The Integral Management of Tao is the method which provides all the essential knowledge and wisdom a human being could possibly possess. In addition, this method is, in the words of Lao Tzu, "simple, easy, and effective." Regardless of who you are, as long as you are the one who wishes to accomplish and establish something meaningful in this world, this book is for you.

The acquisition of the information for *The Integral Management of Tao* was indeed an uneasy task. For example, Sage Kuei Ku's work, *Kuei Ku Tzu*, had been forbidden by feudal lords throughout the millenniums. No one in the ancient or modern world had studied it, written about it, or had access to it, until now. Furthermore, that book was written in a rare form of archaic script. It took me enormous effort to master an ancient language; to read, study, and

PREFACE

decipher the book (I discovered the author had enciphered the text, enormously complicating my task); and to sort all the useful material together. These facts hold true for Yellow Stone Sage's work as well. You will see, as you read this book, that an enormous amount of information is based on the Sages' works. My only humble purpose is to hope you can benefit from it. Your complete achievement is all I am concerned about.

Therefore, dear readers, I repeat Sage Kuei Ku's words to you. Please do not just read the book. Memorize it. Meditate on it. . . . Until you come to a full understanding. It may benefit you a thousand times more. This is the most critical age the world has ever reached. The world needs you and your complete achievement. Thank you and God bless.

> Stephen T. Chang
> May 14, 1988 (Yellow Emperor calender year 4,686)
> San Francisco, California, USA

INTRODUCTION

Let us begin with a story.

One misty morning in the year 1,200 B.C., an Immortal called his disciple to him and said, "Shang, you have followed me for forty years to study Taoism. Now the time has come for you to leave this mountain and meet your destiny, as it is predestined that you will accomplish a great mission. Great honor, wealth and fame await you. Therefore, for your evolution, I must ask you to leave."

The overwhelmed Chiang, Shang pleaded, "Oh! Your Eminence, please do not send me away! Fame and wealth were not my goals when I sought your guidance. My only desire was to follow you to gain eternal wisdom. Everything you have taught me puts to shame all the worldly wealth and luxuries, which are as ephemeral as the mist and unworthy of my time and effort."

Introduction

"Nevertheless, your future has been predetermined; you have an obligation to accomplish this mission. After the deed is done you may return to this mountain and gain your immortality. Now you must leave for your time has come." Those were the Immortal's last words.

Alone, Chiang, Shang struggled down the steep mountainside and headed for the capital of the Yin-Shang Dynasty, where he once lived. There he found his one and only friend, Sung, Yi-Ren who welcomed him to his home as a brother. Sung, a merchant, longed to see Chiang's tremendous learning in application, but Chiang's stay proved to be uneventful, even though much time had passed. Then one day Sung introduced the 72-year-old Chiang to a friend's daughter, 68-year-old Miss Ma. They fell in love, married, and both continued to live under Sung's roof until one day she said, "Shang, you cannot go on relying on your friend however deep your friendship. You should start your own business."

So they moved to their own house and started a bamboo-weaving business. Their goods were hauled to market everyday by Chiang, but no one bought anything. Moneyless, Chiang could not afford to eat. Gnawed by hunger and crippled by fatigue and the summer heat, he always struggled home to complaints from his wife.

Learning of the couple's hardships, Sung rushed over to their house and proposed a more profitable, less grueling business of milling and noodle making. He even forwarded some capital. But just as they were about to receive a return on their investments, the rains came, humidifying the flour and rotting the noodles. This angered Chiang's wife further.

Undeterred, and still hoping to see Chiang's tremendous knowledge in application, Sung then suggested making and selling soy bean curds—a dietary staple and source of steady income. But just as Chiang carried his first batch to market, the winds came, stirring up the dust that soiled and destroyed yet another cash investment.

(This latest failure came to symbolize great adversity; to this

INTRODUCTION

day, people still sumup their descriptions of hardship with four words: *like Chiang, selling tofu*.)

Several business failures later, his wife was unable to contain her despair any longer: "I believed you were a wise man, since you studied so long with a Taoist Immortal. Now I know you're completely useless!"

Chiang was very depressed. Sung again came to comfort him with another, better business proposal. This time he lent Chiang some money to start a sheep and cattle trading business. With these funds Chiang went to the countryside and bought many sheep and cattle. As he drove them to the city to sell, a robbery occurred within the city. The police, in league with the robbers, pretended to give chase and ran into Chiang and all his sheep and cattle. Instead of passing on, they killed the helpless animals and brandished their bloodied swords all the way back to the city, shouting all the while about the strength and heroism they displayed in their complete defeat of the robbers. Of course, the real criminals were never caught. Chiang came home with empty hands, greatly frightened and saddened by the slaughter.

Sung again came and tried to soothe him, but could not refrain from asking, "I'm not trying to be critical, but have you learned anything that could be of use not only to yourself but to others as well?"

"The magnitude of what I've learned defy description," replied Chiang. "My knowledge of human matters is all-encompassing."

"Knowing so much surely you must understand human matters, solve mundane problems, counsel people in their distress?"

"Yes!" Chiang exclaimed suddenly enlightened. "That is what I shall do." With so much experience behind him, and a little help from Sung, Chiang was able to set up a counseling service.

At that period in time, the kingdom was in turmoil. The king and his administration were thoroughly corrupt. Involved in every criminal activity imaginable, they ran up an astronomical deficit and

INTRODUCTION

taxed and exploited the peasants until they were unemployed, homeless, and starving. Campaigns were waged against other kingdoms. Violence and crime were rampant. Life was livable only where Chiang was present, for his services as a consultant benefited and comforted many people.

Chiang's fame spread quickly until it reached the ears of the king. The king summoned Chiang to his court, and, court amenities aside, turned to the subject at hand: "The people seem to revere you and disobey me. I want a grand pavilion with marble pillars and engraved beams covered in gold to be built within thirty years. I want to hire you to oversee the carpenters and peasant workers. You will be awarded with a position in government."

Hearing this Chiang angrily replied, "How can you think of building a pleasure palace when people are starving on the streets? If you proceed according to plan, you will have to tax them even more. And when they are dying from starvation they will not follow my orders to build a pavilion. You should think of improving the economy and putting food into people's stomachs first."

At that the king became displeased and dismissed him. At home his wife railed, "You fool! Finally a chance for you to become somebody and a chance for me to have a future comes within reach, and you blundered it all away. You can't do anything right!"

"Wife, you are short-sighted," replied Chiang. "I cannot scheme against the people. I advised the king to consider his subjects for his own benefit."

This final disagreement caused his wife to divorce him, even as, unknown to them both, word of Chiang's righteousness and wisdom spread until it reached every corner of the country. But then the king's advisors warned, "Your Majesty, this man who steals the hearts of the people is extremely dangerous. He can turn them against you. It is therefore wise to silence him."

Word of ensuing danger reached Chiang, forcing the eighty-year-old man to escape far to the west, towards the tiny kingdom

Introduction

called Chi, where there was reputed to reside a wise and just lord. Near the kingdom, he stopped at a river and did nothing but fish with a straightened hook. (He was not fishing for fish, as it would soon be revealed.) Just as he planned, the lord of Chi and his entourage arrived shortly to seek Chiang's services as chief advisor and counselor and commander in chief. At Chiang's acceptance, the lord himself helped Chiang into his ornamented carriage, took the reins, and led the carriage all the way back to his fortress on foot. (This act became an important and lasting—still repeated after more than three thousand years—ceremonial ritual for inducting a revered manager.) Nine years later, through Chiang's singular planning and commanding expertise, the lord of Chi (King Wu) conquered a vast portion of the continent and established the Chou Dynasty, which was to last eight hundred years and be singularly responsible for setting the foundations for the development of the arts and sciences. No other empire in human history matched its duration. After accomplishing his deed and being ennobled, Chiang returned to his mountain home. To this day, traditional Chinese households continue to pay homage to him, especially during new year celebrations, by displaying the calligraphic symbols meaning "The Great Duke Chiang Who Gives Absolute Freedom is Here."

This story's purpose is to illustrate the following principles:

1) managerial expertise is greatly valued as a catalyst for positive change.

2) all managers must master the lessons of their extensive formal educations and the lessons of life. Thereafter, according to Taoist management theories, potential scars become stars, for all adversity and stress turn into enduring success at their touch. How that is done will be discussed in detail later.

Introduction

THE TAO OF MANAGEMENT

In the latter centuries of the Chou Dynasty, power was decentralized and distributed among numerous feudalities, which later fused into seven major kingdoms after much struggle. Each and every one of the remaining kingdoms sought the common goals of wealth and strength. (In many respects the evolutionary pattern of the kingdom prefigures that of current corporations.) In the pursuit of these goals, there arose in every kingdom a great need for managerial expertise, a need that generated nine different schools with nine different managerial theories and styles. The nine styles are summarized as follows:

I. STYLE OF THE SCHOLAR

Founded by Confucius, this style emphasized order as the most important basis for management. Under this major premise, absolute loyalty was assumed to be the basis for order. It followed that all managers, whether "princes" or "ministers," were motivated out of absolute loyalty to each other and their organization to subordinate individual needs and do everything necessary to assure the organization's success. For when the organization benefited, every member benefited; and when achievement, honor, failure, or shame was experienced by one member, it was experienced by all. Such demands for loyalty were not unlike the demands made by the family. Even the moral codes used by the organization to engender and enforce loyalty paralleled those used by the family. So managers were conditioned for absolute loyalty since childhood. It was thought that children who showed promise (who grew up to be loyal

INTRODUCTION

to their superiors and king) were those who excelled at learning moral codes and being loyal to their elders. Hence the proverb: A loyal minister comes from a filial son. The Scholarly Style was the prevailing managerial style in almost every dynasty for thousands of years, even though experience proved it defective. In reality, the ideal of an orderly, efficient organization welded together by absolute loyalty is illusory and impossibly hard to realize, because true loyalty is almost impossible to achieve. Instead of functioning as a problem solving, success-oriented force, the managerial team turns into an efficient mechanism for smokescreening inefficiency, scandal and corruption. An in depth analysis follows in later chapters.

II. LEGALIST STYLE

Advocates of this style rejected the dependency upon empty, impractical concepts of absolute loyalty in favor of concrete, unshakable laws or rules. These were further enforced by a system of rewards and punishments. Such a system ensured undeviating adherence to laws and rules, or specific duties and procedures, to maximize efficiency and prevent and ferret out inefficiency and corruption. But this management style also had defects. The unrelenting enforcement tactics and strictness involved made the style inhumane. Not only were those tactics psychologically and physically taxing for the entire organization, but they were also ineffective in the end. To determine whether rewards or punishments were merited, reams of data were gathered on employees and then interpreted. Usually rewards or punishments were distributed regardless of the fact that interpretations may have been biased by personal viewpoints. And those who did the reporting were rewarded while those who did the work were punished. The result: resentment and

INTRODUCTION

harsher punishments. As punishments lost their intimidating qualities, managers would explore the entire gamut of punishments, each harsher than the last, until the severest punishment remaining was death. But when death was no longer feared, all was lost. When taken to extremes, the Legalist Style became another form of fascism and was despised for its inhumanity.

III. MO STYLE

The word *mo* means "ink." Laborers use the word *mo* to describe how their complexions have been darkened by their labors under the sun. This style advocated employee rights, for the belief that sincere efforts to secure their health, happiness, comfort, and prosperity would be rewarded with the kind of cooperation and integrity of work that would propel everyone to success. The success and welfare of employees directly affected the success and welfare of the organization. It was considered wise to remove any employee grievances that affected performance negatively by meeting employee demands. Throughout the centuries, the demands have been for non-discrimination of class, creed, sex, race, area, distance, etc.—in other words, complete equality. Specific demands included the right to equal opportunity, to form unions, to on-the-job training, and so on. Fulfillment of these demands was based on love; as long as everyone loved each other and did everything for and with love, everything would be accomplished. However, for various reasons, leaders of political, economic, or other organizations were discouraged from utilizing this style.

Introduction

IV. STYLE OF PRODUCTIVITY

According to productivity theories, exercises in love, laws, moral codes, etc. were exercises in futility; only the full application of human resources served the realization of wealth and strength. Allowing any waste in human resources—that is, lack of production from any segment of society—was considered a crime. No one was exempted from work—not even the prince, who must work harder than others to set an example. Those who chose not to contribute would not qualify for anything. For example, the prince who neglected his duties would be promptly stripped of his rights to food, power, etc. Without exception, every man, woman, and child proved their worth by their level of productivity and earned their keep. That was the purpose of management: to mobilize everyone for work and maintain a high level of productivity (in agriculture, industry, etc.). Only then could goals be reached. But then problems arose. Those who struggled to complete their tasks were rewarded as hard workers, whereas their swifter counterparts were punished as idlers. Productivity in terms of tasks completed declined when people began to devise ways of appearing to be busy instead of actually being busy. Moreover, inundating everyone with work, deadlines, etc. caused everyone to lose sight of the overall direction or goal. As a consequence, even though the organization was headed in the wrong direction, no one was able to catch the mistake before irreparable damage occurred.

V. STYLE OF COMMUNICATION

Adherents of this style reasoned that successful management lay not in engaging in blind, wasted action or exemplifying good working habits, but in devising plans and directing and inspiring their execution through effective communication. Once employees understood what was expected of them and were persuaded by the effective use of language to complete their duties, the goals of wealth and strength could be attained. To ensure true understanding (what was communicated was exactly what was understood), the manager must have complete mastery over thought processes, grammar, terminology, persuasive abilities, etc. Logic in language was imperative. If employee duties were not clarified through effective communication, then the inevitable confusion that resulted would cause mistakes and thus generate ill will. Hence, ambiguity in communication was viewed with the greatest apprehension. A measure taken to prevent and remedy ambiguity was to establish clear lines of communication both vertically and horizontally, between and among princes and ministers. The greatest problem with this style was that arguments over the selection or formation of appropriate words, terminologies, sentence constructions, etc. easily sidetracked managers from their goals.

VI. STYLE OF MILITARISM

Like Sun Tzu, author of the famous book *The Art of War*, proponents of this style said that in obtaining goals of strength and wealth, nothing was as efficient or effective as the use of arms and armed forces. Instead of approaching goals in an oblique, time-consuming manner, one would use armed forces to strike directly at the heart of one's objectives. On the battlefield, one could scheme and plot, use any plan, tactic, strategy . . . whatever was handy, to defend oneself and overcome the opponent and forcibly attain one's goals. Managers needed to know nothing more. Although results were immediate, they were not for the long term benefit and profit of either side. One might be a victorious conqueror but the losses could overshadow the gains. The pages of history abound with the tragedies of war. Lao Tzu said, "Wherever the army has passed, briars and thorns spring up. Years of hunger follow in the wake of a great war." Even Sun Tzu himself said, "Conquering the people's hearts is more effective than occupying their cities."

VII. STYLE OF DIPLOMACY

To adherents of this style, goals of wealth and strength were best attained through diplomatic means, namely, negotiation. Money, justice, prestige, love—everything was negotiable, as they said. Many ventured as far as to say that negotiation was management. One used plots, schemes, strategies, tactics . . . whatever was necessary to reach goals. But in this case the weapon was the tongue. Not only was there no bloodshed, but success was guaranteed at very little expense, whatever one's objectives. However, this style was not free from defects. There was no firm basis upon which long term plans could be set, because everything changed with a twist of the tongue. Negotiation was compromise, and too much compromise became in some cases tripping stones that hindered the attainment of true objectives. In some cases, leaderships were compromised. In others, directions were compromised.

VIII. STYLE OF YIN AND YANG

According to the Universal Law of Cause and Effect, an effect is the direct result of a cause; therefore, everything happens because it is supposed to happen. Cause and effect are represented by the concepts Yin and Yang. As results of efforts to analyze all possible kinds of cause-effect interactions occurring in this universe, certain theories arose, such as: If one strove in the wrong direction, one failed; and if one strove too much, one also failed. People would not have to confront problems of their own creation, if they stopped interfering with the natural laws. God's plans for the universe should not be contended with, nor should God's achievements be claimed as one's own. From these theories arose a "laid-back" style of management. But problems developed when some opportunists overlooked the fact that human input was needed to bring God's plans for humanity into fruition, and used the theories to justify their laziness and their avoidance of responsibilities. Some even tried to excuse their failures or shortcomings as the will of God. Even worse, some used the theories to excuse criminal acts. Because they thought they were not responsible for their actions, they had license to commit any kind of sin they wish. Certain religious fanatics rose to power by taking full advantage of such reasoning to attract a following and engage in immoral or criminal activities.

IX. STYLE OF TAO

Considered to be the highest form of management, it provided the means for utilizing all the preceding eight styles for maximum managerial effectiveness. It also provided the means to nullify the negative aspects of each style automatically. In simplest terms, the Style of Tao is the style of water. Water is used by Lao Tzu to describe the nature of Tao because it has these properties:

A. Besides being self-propelling, water also carries other objects along its currents—it moves others to action.

B. When it meets resistance or obstacles, its power increases.

INTRODUCTION

When fast-flowing water hits an obstacle, all of its energy is completely converted to impact the obstacle with immense force.

C. Water unceasingly searches and wears away rock or land (steadfast obstacles) for new avenues or paths (new opportunities).

D. Water unceasingly cleanses everything in contact with filth, but its cleansing power never diminishes (it always retains its cleansing power, so it is forever improving itself and others).

E. Water flows in rivers and streams to the sea, where it evaporates to form the clouds, from which it is released over land, on which it gathers again into rivers and streams that again flow into the sea. No matter how it changes, it neither loses itself nor its beneficence and efficiency.

About Tao there will be extensive explanations.

It is apparent that the shortcomings of each style generated another style until there were a total of nine at the apex of evolution. Through their influence, Chinese culture developed and matured.

Figure 1.1 The Nine Styles of Management.

PART I

BASIC KNOWLEDGE

Chapter 1

The Tao of Evolution

Life is to live. Life is also to evolve. Anything having a form in this universe has the purpose of using space and time to improve itself and evolve into a higher form. There are five kingdoms in this universe, four of which are visibly living: the Kingdom of Minerals, the Kingdom of Vegetation, the Kingdom of Animals, the Kingdom of Humankind, and the Kingdom of God. The members of each kingdom exist to improve themselves in order to evolve into a higher kingdom.

I. KINGDOM OF MINERALS

This Kingdom encompasses all mineral formations, from the tiniest grain of sand to the largest planet and galaxy in the universe.

Though not readily perceptible, members of this kingdom go through "life cycles" of generation, maturation, and degeneration. Each has a "life cycle" unique to its kind, and each serves a particular purpose, as shown by the findings of astronomists, astrophysicists, geologists, geomorphologists, minerologists, and so on. As has been further demonstrated, mineral formations are capable of absorbing, processing, and emitting energy in the form of light, sound, heat, magnetism, etc.—the most basic processes of life. Where there is change, there is life (no matter how basic) and evolution.

II. KINGDOM OF VEGETATION

The members of this Kingdom, which include viruses and bacteria, have in addition to physical forms physical senses. Their sole purpose is to reproduce. They have no creativity and are incapable of intentionally benefiting other organisms in any way, though the purposes they serve are vitally important. Such physical bodies also live to evolve.

III. KINGDOM OF ANIMALS

The members of this Kingdom have, in addition to physical bodies with physical senses, mental bodies. Found here are the first expressions of thought, will, and emotion. A dog, for instance, has a mind that is capable of responding to its owner's commands and demonstrating the rudiments of learning. But one cannot expect more from animals, for they lack spiritual bodies. Animals always live and reproduce in accordance with certain timetables. They mechanically follow universal laws, do not have the desire or the drive to progress beyond their present conditions, and do not possess the creative abilities associated with this desire. Animals lack this desire because they lack a spiritual body.

IV. KINGDOM OF HUMANKIND

The members of this Kingdom possess, in addition to physical and mental bodies, spiritual bodies.

Where there is spirit, there is hope and creativity. And because the spirit is not limited by space or time and the body is, a sense of incompleteness arises, along with a desire to progress beyond the present physical condition. Hopes that are beyond the limits of space and time imbue man with the urge and ability to create. So man, hoping his creations will somehow make his physical presence last as long as his spiritual presence, created religion, science, music, literature and art, erected monuments of lasting materials, and even built empires.

But none of his accomplishments have ever given him enough satisfaction; at the root of all his travails, man desires to be immortal. (Religions partially satisfy the desire for immortality, but they focus on life after death.) So, unsatisfied desires still fill the hearts of men and women with frustration and pain.

Taoist scholars have always understood the true meaning of man's desire for immortality. They have known man's desire to enter the Kingdom of God to be the true goal of evolution. Consequently, they have devised methods for walking with God, spiritualizing the body, and lifting man into the fifth kingdom as he lives on earth.

V. THE KINGDOM OF GOD

This Kingdom can be reached. In this kingdom the human body is spiritualized. When you are a spiritualized being, unlimited by space or time, you have access to all corners of the universe. A spiritual, or immortal, being experiences complete satisfaction, peace and happiness, since he or she is in unity with God and the universe.

Not all human beings are qualified to enter the Kingdom of God. According to Taoist scholars, there are four classes of human beings in the Kingdom of Humankind, and they are (in ascending order): Evil Men, Little Men, Gentlemen, and Sages. Only Sages are qualified to evolve into the Kingdom of God.

The Kingdom of God itself is divided into three classes of *Hsien*, or "Immortals," and they are (in ascending order): *Ren Hsien*, or "Transformed Immortal"; *Ti Hsien*, or "Terrestrial Immortal"; and *Tien Hsien*, or "Celestial Immortal." So there must first be "promotion among the ranks" before there is evolution to a higher kingdom.

As evolution is a continuous process, there will forever be many kingdoms and classes of life existing together.

A. Evil Men are only human in form, as they are still animalistic in nature. Their evolution into the Kingdom of Humankind is incomplete, since they do not understand or appreciate morality or propriety. Entertainment, contention, consumption, and reproduction, the four basic instincts, preoccupy their daily lives. In most societies this group is controlled by force, because they are capable of murder, rape, and other evil crimes.

B. Little Men are unwise, limited in abilities, and have evil patterns of thought. Everything done by this group is done for short-sighted gains. Members of this group are capable of scheming and cheating for useless, unimportant things. Their concerns and their lives are petty. They are too cowardly to commit overt crimes (intentions are always disguised) and too limited to help society in a grand way. Little Men are effectively controlled by laws in most societies.

C. Gentlemen understand and pursue morality, propriety, and cultivation of abilities, for they are guided by propriety and reason. They desire enlightenment for themselves and other human beings. When the members of this group increase in number, society flourishes. When their numbers diminish, society suffers.

D. Sages are those who truly understand and pursue righteousness. These individuals work to improve and enlighten human beings and create a peaceful world through the spread of harmony and true knowledge. Sages are guided by righteousness.

E. Transformed Immortals are cultivators of Taoism. Being wise, holy, and kind, these individuals are involved in improving world affairs. Upon death, their physical bodies are resurrected. Love is the guiding force of these immortals.

F. The Terrestrial Immortal is a Taoist who, being extremely wise, holy, and ego-less, has left behind all human characteristics. The immortal survives for centuries and is involved in altering world events, for he has the experience of accomplishing many great deeds. Perfect virtue is his guiding force.

G. A Celestial Immortal is a Taoist who has survived for thousands of years and has accomplished great deeds too numerous to name. The body of the Celestial Immortal is completely spiritualized (not limited by space or time). The Celestial Immortal and God are one. Here, Tao is the guiding force.

Each member of each of these seven classes has a physical, mental, and spiritual body—the three folds of the body. The differences between each class lie in the degree of dominance one particular body has over the others. For example, for Evil Men the physical body dominates the mental and spiritual bodies. For Sages the mental body dominates the other bodies. For Celestial Immortals the spiritual body dominates the other bodies.

The physical body is governed by four basic instincts: entertainment, contention, consumption, and reproduction. The physical body can be represented by a square:

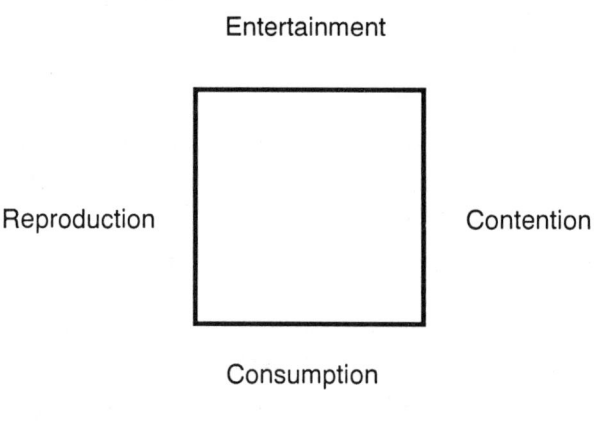

Figure 1.2

The mental body can be represented by a triangle, because of three faculties: thought, emotion, and will.

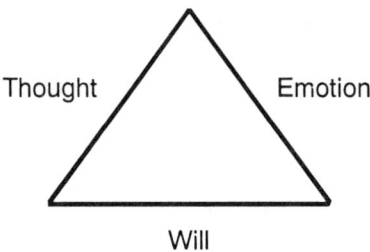

Figure 1.3

The spiritual body can be represented by a circle, because it is not limited by space or time. It has a conscience, possesses flawless intuition, and communicates with God.

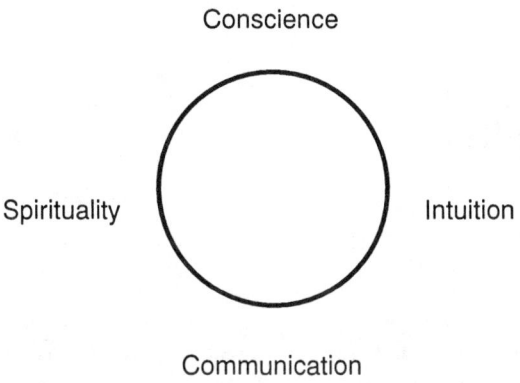

Figure 1.4

Ideally the physical and mental bodies should be subservient to the spiritual body. The spiritual body should send orders to the mental body, which determines the proper method for bringing these orders into fruition. The mental body then guides the physical body in carrying out these plans. Every activity is based on foresight, wisdom, and conscience, and every activity conforms to the ways of God.

The Tao of Evolution

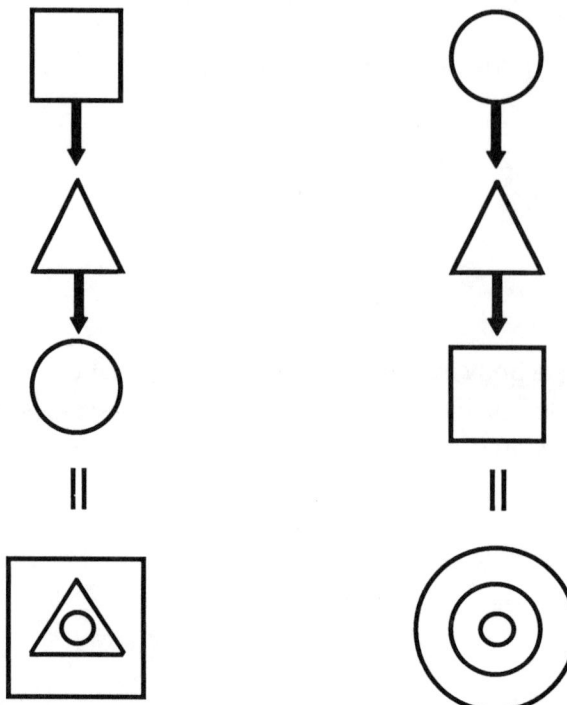

Figure 1.5 Order of Influence (Incorrect)

Figure 1.6 Order of Influence (Correct)

Unfortunately this is rarely the case. Instead we frequently find that the physical body has repressed the spiritual body and enslaved the mental body. The physical needs for play, violence, food, and sex forces the mental body to contrive ways to satisfy, excuse, even sanction these primal needs. This complete reversal of the true order results in all the miseries of this world. "When Tao is lost," explained Lao Tzu, "human beings take up virtue; when virtue is lost, human beings insist on love; when love is lost, people demand righteousness; when righteousness is lost, people rely on propriety; when propriety is lost, law is sought; but when law is lost, force is sought; and when force is sought, all traces of civilization are lost."

THE TAO OF EVOLUTION

Fortunately we have been given the tools—the techniques of Taoism—for chiseling a circle out of a crude square:

Figure 1.7

The practice of Taoism accelerates evolutionary advancement by helping mankind accumulate good deeds in the most efficient way possible—without martyrdom. According to Pao Pu Tzu, 200 good deeds are required to become a Transformed Immortal, 300 good deeds are required to become a Terrestrial Immortal, and 1200 good deeds are required to become a Celestial Immortal. Good deeds are defined as actions that benefit oneself as well as others. Actions that hurt one party while benefiting another are undesirable. Actions that hurt both parties are least desirable; one such transgression can nullify all of the good deeds that have been accumulated and can cause evolutionary retrogression as a result.

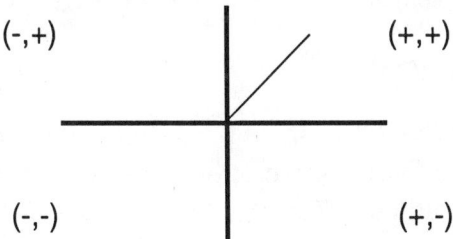

(+,+) = Good deeds (everyone benefits)
(-, -) = Harmful deeds (everyone is hurt)
(+, -) = Partially good deeds (others benefit; the self is sacrificed)
(-,+)=Partially harmful deeds (others are hurt; the self benefits)

Figure 1.8

The Tao of Evolution

Lao Tzu described our every action as being recorded and computed by the stars, which are governed by the North Star. The formulas for accomplishing many deeds are revealed in this book, as are the secrets of securing a long-lived and properly functioning physical body, without which few deeds can be accomplished (see Appendix). That is why martyrdom is regarded with great reservation; it cuts off the flow of benefits to society and retards evolutionary advancement by destroying the physical agent through which deeds are achieved.

According to the theories of Taoism, associated with every class of human being is a corresponding guiding principle of government. When human beings progress from one class to another, the guiding principle by which they are governed progresses correspondingly. This is an arrangement that assures steady progress until Celestial Immortality and Tao is reached.

Seven Levels of Humankind	Seven Types of Government
Celestial Immortal	Tao
Terrestrial Immortal	Perfect Virtue
Transformed Immortal	Love
Sages	Righteousness
Gentlemen	Propriety
Little Men	Law
Evil Men	Force

Evolution without Taoism is a painfully slow process—it has taken us millions of years of evolution to become what we are today. Incorporating or utilizing Taoist methods of management accelerates evolutionary advancement in the most efficient and beneficial way possible.

This pattern of evolution can be used to give coherence to our past, present, and future.

Human beings began to distinguish themselves from animals when primitive forms of spiritual worship and agriculture were invented. These marked the beginnings of a period that began in the obscure prehistoric past, known as the Age of Evil Men. No matter what stage of development the social, religious, economic, or political systems were in, force was the pervading guiding principle. It brought satisfaction to the four instinctive needs to play, fight, eat, and have sex. To illustrate, we need only remind ourselves of archeological findings or any other record of ancient history to recall the accomplishments achieved through forceful means. They included the slaughter and enslavement of human beings; the building of palaces, temples, hanging gardens, or other structures; proliferation of bacchanals or human sacrifices; proliferation of bloody sports; and so on. Slavery, rape, incest, sacrifice, war, murder, theft, corruption were rarely questioned. If questioned it usually conflicted with other means to the same ends. And whether one particular means superseded the next was determined by force. Those who had or accumulated force enslaved, killed, colonized, and maimed to make the masses function in a particular way. Thus emperors, kings, etc. ruled. Moral standards in general were not high. But in certain recesses of the world's civilizations, advanced stages of evolution had already begun to emerge.

For the majority of the world's civilizations, progress into the Age of Little Men began about the time of the Industrial Revolution. The need for forced labor having been lightened and moral standards having been raised somewhat as a consequence, human beings began to refer to their needs as rights. Though they continued to enslave and kill, rape and maim, debauch and exploit; they justified their actions by declaring and using their rights to fulfill their instinctive needs. For purposes of protecting and enforcing such rights; ideologies, laws, legal and other systems were formed or elaborated upon. The legal system especially proliferated in this age. When interests polarized, the result was conflict. The clash of democratic and socialist interests was one such conflict. Though in the beginning only a few truly advocated true human rights, their numbers began to swell as more and more people began to interpret the declarations of rights and laws literally, resulting in deeper deliberations on issues of human rights, fairness, truth, equality, etc. The search for rights uncovered many instances of inequality; the search for legality, more illegality; for fairness, more unfairness.

Now human beings are in the midst of a transition from the Age of Little Men to the Age of Gentlemen. Fully knowledgeable of past and present wrongs because of technological advances in communication, people of this age seek balance in all aspects of life. They seek social, religious, political and economic balance. As access to information continues to improve and as awareness levels continue to be heightened, the injustices inflicted and tolerated in the past will no longer be tolerated. Gentlemen actively try to right the wrongs of the past. This age is above all an age of propriety and rationality. Because moral consciousness has been elevated still further, people begin to ponder over how they stand in balance with others—especially whether their actions are correct in light of higher moral standards. However, the search for balance and propriety and the influx of unending information will uncover even greater wrongs and imbalances.

Progressing beyond this is the Age of Sages. Righteousness is the guiding principle. In this age, activities and thoughts are centered upon the welfare of others.

And beyond is the Age of Transformed Immortals, the first age of spirituality. Greater responsibilities are assumed. Love is the guiding principle. Egos are no longer involved in the deeds that are done.

Then follows the Age of the Terrestrial Immortals, wherein perfect virtue is the guiding principle. Greater deeds involving heavy responsibilities are accomplished.

The final age is that of the Celestial Immortals. When Tao rules, everything has achieved a state of perfect balance and individual involvement is no longer necessary. True, perpetual bliss is achieved without effort.

Why do we need Taoist management? Since the beginning, whenever or wherever two people have been present, management has been a necessity. Management has always been intimately connected with man's evolution, so nothing is more important to evolution than proper management. Proper management balances all the infinite varieties and stages of life on this planet and allows them to help each other evolve for the benefit of all. That is the universal will, which no one can defy or escape without terrible consequences.

Why be a manager? Again, universal will. Whether you approve or not, you must complete your evolutionary mission. If you fail you will delay your own progress and extend your miseries, which magnify with every lesson badly learned. You are not working for your parents or relatives, teachers or associates, friends or lovers, you are working for your own evolution—and that alone more than fulfills all of their expectations of you.

One day King Wu and Chiang, Shang were conversing when King Wu asked, "Are there any differentiations of leadership?" Chiang replied, "Yes indeed My Lord. There are nine rules [in relative terms]":

> 1. A man with the basic abilities to get up early in the morning and retire late at night will be able to lead his wife and children.
>
> 2. Additional qualities of sympathy (for others) and enthusiasm allow a man to lead ten people.
>
> 3. Adding talent, skill, and communicative abilities to the above abilities allows a man to lead a hundred people.
>
> 4. Additional qualities of honesty, loyalty, and faith allow a man to lead a thousand people.

5. Additional abilities to magnify his studies, formulate his own theories, and understand issues allow a man to lead ten thousand people.

6. Adding to this bravery and the ability to assume great responsibilities and fight for issues allow a man to lead one hundred thousand people.

7. Additional abilities to project humbleness and accept good ideas allow a man to lead a million people.

8. Adding to this good strategy and humanity allow a man to lead several countries.

9. Additional abilities to fight for righteousness and justice allow a man to lead the world.

The human race is a marathon. All of us are automatically entered at birth willing or not. Our birth launched our race, so the only choice we have is to be a winner or a loser. In order to win, given the magnitude of the task, we need rules to train motivation, coordination, direction, inspection, and organization. A detailed discussion of these rules will follow in the next few chapters.

CHAPTER 2

THE TAO OF YIN AND YANG RELATIVISM

According to *The Book of History* (one of the five classics of ancient China and an ancient forerunner of the constitution), the prime minister's first qualification is to know Yin and Yang, and the prime minister's first priority is to adjust Yin and Yang.

There were two golden ages in Chinese history, the Han and T'ang Dynasties. It was during the height of the first golden age, the Han Dynasty, that the responsibilities of the prime minister were fully defined. It was defined by Vice Prime Minister Chen, Ping in answer to one of Emperor Wen's questions: "The job of the prime minister, it is written, is to help the emperor adjust Yin and Yang, ensuring that right actions are taken at right times and ensuring that ministers and officials meet and suit their responsibilities. . . ."

That statement has been praised throughout the centuries by scholars specializing in the study of the constitution, laws, legal systems, and government structure. Consensus established this historical fact to be the case that best exemplified the success achieved through a system that delegated the right authority to the right official. That system was the system of adjusting Yin and Yang.

What is Yin and what is Yang? Why are they so important?

It is stated in the Yellow Emperor's *Classic of the Internal* that the entire universe is an oscillation of the forces Yin and Yang. Within everything in this universe is the constant, dynamic interaction of two distinct, yet inseparable and integral, opposites: Yin and Yang. Taoist scholars have extrapolated from the principles regarding the nature of Yin and Yang that the feminine is Yin and the masculine is Yang. This is how they are symbolized:

Figure 2.1

Deeper investigations revealed that God, life, goodness, justice, righteousness, light, peace, heat, wealth, happiness, heaven, growth . . . the sun, the active, that which is on the surface, are Yang. By inference, Satan, death, evil, injustice, unrighteousness, darkness, war, cold, poverty, unhappiness, hell, decay . . . the moon, the passive, that which is deep or hidden, are Yin. Yin and Yang represent every conceivable pair of opposites: birth and death, growth and decay, health and illness, right and left, front and back sides, positive or negative magnetic poles, etc.

The Tao of Yin and Yang Relativism

Just as we cannot know what heat is if we've never been cold, or what happiness is if we've never been sad, so too Yin and Yang can never exist in total isolation from one another. Each is a different side of the same coin, integral parts of a single entity. Both constantly interact thus. This kind of interaction persists in all things: objects, attitudes, personal characteristics, thoughts, etc. For instance, the two faces of a piece of paper make up one piece of paper. One without the other results in nothingness.

Seen in this light, many supposedly opposite entities and concepts take on new qualities—even God and Satan appear different. If we apply this theory to them, God and Satan become one; one cannot condemn one without condemning the other.

How can this be so? In older versions of the Bible, the first book of the Old Testament was Job, not Genesis. A story about Job was told in this first book. In a dialogue between God and Satan, God praised Job for his faith and righteousness. Satan challenged God, saying that Job's faith, a result of God's gifts, would disappear when the gifts disappeared. God allowed Satan to test Job, and Job suffered many adversities. Seeing that Job's faith was unfaltering, Satan challenged God again, saying that harm inflicted upon Job's person would end his faith. God accepted the challenge and permitted Satan to do his work. Still Job remained steadfast. In this book, God and Satan work together and counsel each other. The trials of Job seem to be caused by Satan, but Satan has God's permission.

Another type of interaction represented by Yin and Yang is that of generation and degeneration. They are as follows:

Generating:
1) Yang generates Yang   3) Yin generates Yang
2) Yin generates Yin   4) Yang generates Yin

Degenerating:
1) Yang degenerates Yang   3) Yin degenerates Yang
2) Yin degenerates Yin   4) Yang degenerates Yin

The Tao of Yin and Yang Relativism

The generating interaction can be understood in terms of the following example. Rampaging criminals cause people to establish a police force to protect themselves. Yin (criminals) is generating Yang (police force) because the police force will not exist if criminals do not force its inception. Gradually the police force grows (Yang generates Yang), and soon it becomes burdensome to support (taxes are raised). Corruption in the police force results in its participation in crimes (Yang generates Yin). Meanwhile, criminal forces grow to counteract the growing police force (Yin generates Yin).

The degenerating interaction can be understood in terms of the following example. When a police force captures a criminal, a Yang-degenerates-Yin interaction takes place. When government cuts the force's funds, a Yang-degenerates-Yang interaction takes place. When its funds are reduced, the force is overcome by criminals, a Yin-degenerates-Yang interaction. The swelling criminal population will then witness territorial disputes that will decrease its numbers, a Yin-degenerates-Yin interaction.

The third type of interaction manifested is that Yin at its most extreme point becomes Yang and Yang at its most extreme point becomes Yin. The day at its greatest extent turns into evening. The night at its greatest extent turns into morning.

The fourth type of interaction is that both Yin and Yang coexist together—has both Yin and Yang natures. Taoist scholars never encourage celebration, because hidden within a happy situation is the seed of sadness. Hidden disasters develop under fortunate circumstances, and good fortune develops under disastrous circumstances.

The fifth type of interaction involves a reciprocal Yin and Yang reaction. An example would be the mutual attraction of the positive and negative poles of a magnet.

The sixth type of interaction illustrates the comparative effects Yin and Yang have upon each other. A motorcycle is bigger than a tricycle; therefore, it is considered to be yang in relation to the

The Tao of Yin and Yang Relativism

tricycle, which is Yin. But compared to a car, the motorcycle is much smaller and is Yin in relation to the car. The car, when compared to a truck, becomes Yin.

So far the relativity of Yin and Yang and the dynamic tension of their interactions are discussed as if they were in a vacuum—that is, isolated from the effects of the environment.

Now further developments upon these basic interactions will be presented in consideration of the external effects of space and time.

Below is a representation of Yin and Yang and the external forces:

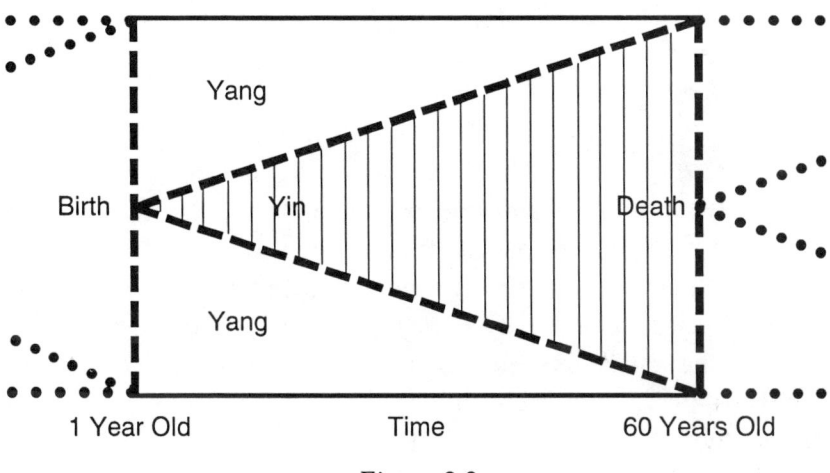

Figure 2.2

We have taken a cross section of a time continuum to see how Yin and Yang interact in a section of time. If we take this section to mean a person's life span, we see that the starting point represents a person's birth and the ending point the moment of death. At the moment of birth, Yang (life) is manifested at full force. But within is buried a seed of Yin. As time passes by, we see that Yin gradually expands in force and gradually displaces the force of Yang. So much so that, at age 60, the forces of Yin (death) completely overwhelm and displace Yang. But within the full manifestation of Yin forces, there is buried a seed of Yang. The expansion of Yin is depicted as gradual and even when in reality it may push aside Yang forces in moments of strength or shrink in moments of weakness (Yang forces may displace Yin forces similarly). If we look beyond this cross section we see that the entire progression begins again.

From these interactions, there arose six Yin-Yang Laws that defined the entire universe.

I. LAW OF CYCLICALNESS (or CAUSE AND EFFECT)

Because Yin and Yang is in everything and because Yin will always revert to Yang and vice versa, the phenomenon of cyclicalness is universal—though the time needed to complete the cycle may vary in every case. Everything in this universe proceeds cyclically. Every day, for as long as we live, the sun will come back to us. Though the sun disappears at night, that does not mean it disappears forever—the Law of Cyclicalness guarantees its reappearance at the proper time. This same law is in effect when, after we sow beans, we reap beans. The same law holds if we sow melons: we reap melons. No matter what we do, good or bad, we can be sure there will be retribution. As Lao Tzu said, "The household that accumulates good deeds must be blessed with happiness, and the household that accumulates evil must be cursed with calamity." Also, in the Classic of Purity, Lao Tzu stated, "There are no special doors for calamity or happiness (in man's lot); they come as men themselves call them. Their recompenses follow good and evil as the shadow follows the substance." The importance of retribution cannot be overemphasized. The manager must consider the aftereffects of any plan or action. He must not be short-sighted and neglect to consider the long term consequences, because short-sighted profit will result in disaster quickly. An all too-often repeated mistake is allowing overeagerness for success blind people to everything except immediate advantages. The results can be devastating (for example, misappropriation and short-sighted agricultural policies can cause worldwide poverty and hunger).

II. LAW OF GROWTH

A condition of Yin or Yang must develop, or grow, until it turns into its opposite condition. The rate of turnover is directly proportional to the rate of a condition's development. So a condition of Yang turns into Yin quickly if the growth rate is great. Therefore, the Law of Growth states that faster growth brings earlier death. This law has numerous connotations. The more one concentrates (pressure, etc.) the earlier the dissolution. We constantly hear of the desire for fast growth, but the problems arising from meteoric growth, whether foreseen or unforeseen, are unsolvable—there is no time for solutions. The more one tries to increase Yang (for example, through heavy exploitation) the more one brings on Yin (for example, poverty and other problems). Everything that was labored for (Yang) will quickly pass away (Yin). Since Yang must turn into Yin, accelerating growth accelerates this turnover, a fact nobody can prevent from happening. Manipulating the natural law will be futile—it is not possible to change a universal law. As Lao Tzu said, "Unless the solution comes first, it is better not to invent." Therefore, we should consider how problems of nuclear wastes may be solved before we compete for superiority in the area of nuclear innovation; otherwise, because of the ambitions of the few, everybody is led to irreversible disaster. The manager must know how to abide by this law.

III. LAW OF LOSS AND GAIN

Since there is Yin in Yang and Yang in Yin, loss or gain is not absolute. According to the Law of Loss and Gain, a superficial loss can be in reality a true gain, and a superficial gain can be in reality a true loss. So Taoist scholars never recognize absolute calamity or happiness for what they seem to be. As Lao Tzu said, "Misery!—happiness is to be found by its side! Happiness!—misery lurks beneath it!"

There is a famous story illustrating this point. About 2,500 years ago, there was a wealthy man who wanted to celebrate his only son's birthday. He bought a pony as a birthday gift to surprise him. During the party, a servant reported that the pony ran away and was lost. The son was so disappointed and miserable that the festive mood was shattered. But a while later, the pony was found and brought back to the son, who was elated. The entire family was elated also. Everyday thereafter, he rode and cared for the pony, until one day, in a riding accident, he seriously injured his leg. Everybody became miserable and wished they had never seen the pony, because the son was handicapped for life. Then one day, an imperial order from the First Emperor of Chin, Chin Shih Huang, came and forced every man in the village—except those who were handicapped or old—to serve in the construction of the Great Wall. Every worker from the village died from the construction; only this lamed son survived. There is no absolute calamity or happiness. So in order to be a good leader, one must be careful to make educational, training, or motivational policies that do not elevate expectations excessively. Over-brightening results causes greater disappointments; consequently, whenever plans are made, take care to consider potential problems in addition to the benefits. Saying something is a panacea for every ill is wrong; problems always exist so one must be prepared. (Unfortunately, the dream for utopia is just that: a dream.) A talented manager must always be prepared for any challenge, since evolution is never-ending.

Dogs fight for things as paltry as a bone; and when one finally dies and the other lies wounded, neither gets the bone. Roosters are said to fight for egos; but in the end when one dies and the other lies wounded, neither benefits from the hard-won ego. Wise men know how to divide their shares.

IV. LAW OF TIME

The progression from Yin to Yang (or vice versa) is dependent upon time; therefore, time is critically important to the condition of Yin and Yang. Time cannot be controlled by man, so man cannot withhold time. Spring inevitably changes to summer; summer, to winter, and so on—nothing can be withheld. Spring has its utility; summer, its own. Every season fulfills its purpose within a specified time frame. Everybody has his own mission and is endowed with the talent for accomplishing this mission, but the accomplishment of that mission is dependent upon time. Most people do not realize that they have done their best in the time that has been given, and they neglect to move ahead onto other missions. If excuses are used to hold onto present conditions, the ways of others are blocked. A leader must understand the limits time places on the accomplishments of missions and move himself and others ahead, so that upon accomplishment no one will block the path of others. Otherwise, a possessive attitude toward a position will block all progress, the greatest crime from the standpoint of Taoism. A great leader must know his own mission and timing—the time to get in and the time to get out—otherwise, his great success will turn sour. As Lao Tzu said, "When the work is done, and one's name is becoming distinguished, to withdraw into obscurity is the way of heaven." Most people would say, "I worked for it ... it's MINE ... I deserve to hold onto it forever...." These people will lose everything in the end. If, for example, George Washington insisted on becoming a king, held onto his position until his death, and passed his power to his progeny, his success and good name would not be so lasting. Furthermore, any one thing will develop an opposite, and any pair of opposites will come together in the end. As King Solomon said in Ecclesiastes 3:1-8, "To every *thing there is* a season, and a time to every purpose under the heaven: A time to be born, and a time to die ... A time to kill, and a time to heal ... A time to love, and a time to hate; a time of war, and a time of peace." From an enlarged viewpoint, the more foolishness there is, the more hate and war there are—this is Yin. The more wisdom there is, the more love, peace, and integrity there are—this is Yang. Because time will definitely show what condition it is. Even time itself is subject to Yin-Yang transformations. As Saint Peter said in Peter 3:8, "One day *is* with God as a thousand years, and a thousand years as one day." Transformations between Yin and Yang takes countless forms and infinite time. The meanings are beyond the vocabularies of human language. Taoist scholars say one has to meditate upon these meanings until one comes to a full realization.

V. THE LAW OF UTILITY

All members of the three kingdoms before man follow the basic interactions of Yin and Yang mechanically; only man is capable of adjusting them according to his will and talent. But the Kingdom of

The Tao of Yin and Yang Relativism

Humankind is itself split into two divisions: those who are managed by Yin-Yang Laws and interactions, and those who manage Yin-Yang Laws and interactions. Those who can utilize or manage Yin-Yang Laws have a life guaranteed by success. An example of this management is given by Lao Tzu: "When he is going to [despoil] something from another, he will first have made gifts to him." From his words arose a technique: to get from others, one must first give. Giving is Yin, getting is Yang. In this case Yin has been turned into Yang—the best technique of gain. Man knows he cannot just charge ahead and get what he wants; he must use the strategy of gain, a form of compromise. Lao Tzu also said, "May not the TAO (WAY) of HEAVEN be compared to the (method of) bending a bow? The (part of the bow) which was high should be brought low, and what was low should be raised up. . . . It is the WAY of HEAVEN to diminish superabundance, and to supplement deficiency." High is Yang, low is Yin; superabundance is Yang, deficiency is Yin. Compromise between these extremes is the way of adjusting Yin and Yang. Details will be given later regarding this principle.

VI. LAW OF IMPERFECTION

100 percent perfection does not exist in the real world. The best one can do is hope to come close to it. Perfection is either in the past or in the future or in the dream world. Because inside Yang there must be Yin—nothing is absolute. Nothing, for example, is absolutely good or bad. Therefore tolerance is a necessary strategy.

From these six Laws of Yin and Yang, the basic philosophy of the Integral Management of Tao arose. Knowledge of these laws qualifies a prime minister for his post. If he knows and utilizes these well, then he is good prime minister.

The Tao of Yin and Yang Relativism

After we have come to know the Laws of Yin and Yang, we will learn about its use. This book is to emphasize the practical ways of utilizing the Laws of Yin and Yang.

And before we do so, let me acquaint you with an important Taoist sage, who was known only as Kuei Ku Tzu, or Sage of the Valley of the Ghost (about 300 B.C.–). He was a very learned philosopher and teacher, and many students went to Kuei Ku, or Ghost Valley, to study with him. Four of them became very famous because their training helped them alter history. Two were Pang, Chuen and Sun, Pin (very famous military strategists and authors of books called *The Art of War*). The other two—Chang, Yi and Su, Chin—were, respectively, a great statesman and a great prime minister. Part of every student's training involved a final examination, during which Sage Kuei Ku had his students climb into a deep pit and asked them to construct speeches that incorporated everything he had taught them. Their objective was to move Sage Kuei Ku deeply enough to lower the ladder so they may climb out. Su, Chin was the student who not only convinced the Sage to lower the ladder, but also moved him to tears. Those who failed did not graduate and had to begin their studies again. But those who graduated were given an analysis of their futures by the Sage before they set out into the world. Nothing in the universe escaped Sage Kuei Ku's comprehension; not even the destinies of his students.

The following story, that of Su, Chin's path to glory, exemplifies the penetration of Sage Kuei Ku's knowledge. When Su, Chin was leaving the school at Kuei Ku to begin job hunting, Sage Kuei Ku handed him a book entitled *Kuei Ku Tzu,* saying, "I am entrusting you with the secret knowledge herein. If you fail to gain employment you shall study this book again and again until your very soul pulsates with its words. In the end your success will be immense." Having bid farewell to the Sage, Su headed for the strongest and wealthiest Kingdom of Chin to try to gain employment. He tried for several months without success. Penniless and dejected he returned to his humble home, where he received no welcome from his parents, brother, or spouse. All of them disapproved of his desire to hold a high government position, because they needed him to do farm work. He ran to the river and was about to commit suicide when the memory of the Sage's words rescued him. He immediately went home to study the book with determined diligence until he came to a full realization of every word in the book. That came only after a year of hard studying, wherein he gave himself no rest. To keep his head from tilting off to sleep, he tied his hair to the ceiling with a rope. Even then he still had to stab himself awake with an awl, disregarding the blood that flowed from the wound. (To this day, his actions are recalled when students need encouragement to study hard.) When he felt he was ready, he borrowed some funds from his brother and resumed his search. This time he succeeded and became the prime minister of six kingdoms at the same time. This is like being the CEO of six of the largest corporations at the same time. No other example like his can be found in the entirety of human history. He was also the founder of the Style of Communication.

In his book, Sage Kuei Ku called Yin-Yang the first knowledge of every phenomenon in the universe and the entrance to all existence.

He defined Yang as life, happiness, rejoicing, wealth, status, honor, glory, fame, love, favor, gain, pride, facility, reward, hope, victory, blessing . . . beginnings. And Yin as death, sadness, lamentation, poverty, lowness, dishonor, condemnation, namelessness, hate, disfavor, loss, humility, difficulty, punishment, despair, failure, calamity . . . endings.

"From the beginning, the Sages were always way ahead of the others because they were the ones who truly understood Yin-Yang, melded to it, transformed it into a two-edged sword, discerned the thoughts and intentions of the heart, and then made it into an incomparable power. Consequently, achievements were quick, tremendous, remarkable, and unshakable."

CHAPTER 3

THE TAO OF EIGHT ATTITUDES

The right person, who does the right thing, in the right way, at the right place, with the right people, commands success.

Who is the right person? Am I? I must be. . . . Why and what can I be?

How often do you hear: "You can have anything in this world. . . . Everybody is equally gifted. . . . All the talents are within you already; all you have to do is to let them out. . . . All you need is ambition, enthusiasm, positive thinking. . . . You do not have to do a thing; God will do everything for you if you are chosen. . . ." These words are spoken to provide inspiration and encouragement. Unfortunately, they do not furnish any practical methods for fulfilling their promises and, as a consequence, only serve to heighten expectations. These expectations create over-inflated egos, which in turn cause over-inflated ambitions. Gigantic egos limit the capacity to learn, to understand and correct one's limitations, and to handle greater responsibilities. When gigantic egos are coupled with gigantic ambitions, they cause endless frustration and depression, mental illness, crime, and so on.

Taoism teaches us that everybody comes to earth to accomplish his mission. This is a fact regardless of a person's awareness or willingness to comply. What is exactly meant by "accomplish"? By "mission"? Accomplish simply means starting, growing, and finishing. Mission simply means learning, training, and achieving. Very few of us are born naturally knowing how; most of us need to learn and undergo training. A willingness to learn leads to earlier understanding; a willingness to train leads to earlier accomplishments. The more learned and trained a person is, the more important his missions become. Without exception, the Cause-Effect Law assures that rewards come with proper achievements and punishments come with unpreparedness. It was to help people learn and train that the special science of Taoism was developed.

To understand the system let us return to Yin-Yang again, to gain insight from a different perspective. This time Yin and Yang will be used in an algebraic formula:

$$(a + b)^3 = a^3 + 3a^2b + 3ab^2 + b^3$$

Let a = — (Yang)
Let b = - - (Yin),
then

$$(a + b)^3 \text{ or } (— + - -)^3 =$$

$$a^3 \quad + \quad 3a^2b \quad + \quad 3ab^2 \quad + \quad b^3$$

Trigrams

THE TAO OF EIGHT ATTITUDES

Eight "trigrams" are produced. Taoist scholars have assigned manifold attributes to each trigram, so that they may reflect phenomena such as cosmic phenomena, directional phenomena, etc. In this chapter we will deal only with the cosmic and directional phenomena.

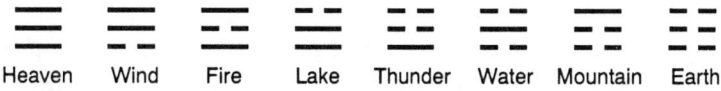

Figure 3.1 Cosmic Phenomena

The cosmic phenomena associated with and symbolized by the eight trigrams are shown above. The proper sequence in which they are read should be: heaven, water, mountain, thunder, wind, fire, earth, and lake.

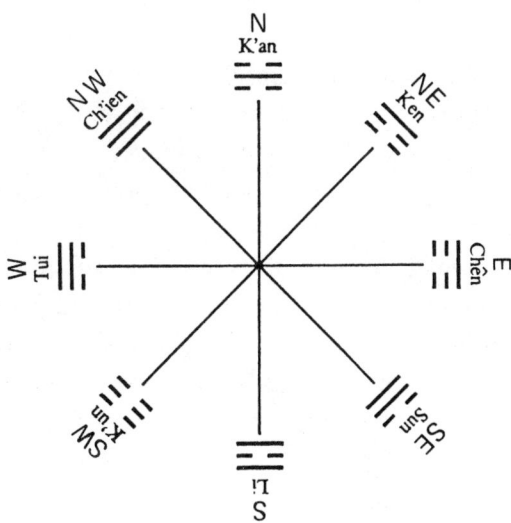

Figure 3.2 Directional Phenomena

The Tao of Eight Attitudes

Directional phenomena are also associated with and symbolized by the trigrams. On earth, we orient ourselves by designating directions. Taoist scholars divided the directions into eight major directions: north, south, east, west, northeast, northwest, southeast, and southwest. Then they assigned a trigram to each direction, resulting in the association illustrated by Figure 3.2 on the previous page.

Through a long process of logical deduction, it has been determined that the previous pattern is read clockwise beginning at the heaven, northwest, or first trigram and ending at the lake, west, or eighth trigram.

Most of the above associations were established by studies conducted during the Fu Hsi Dynasty (about 3,000 B.C.). Directional associations came later when King Wen, founding father of the Chou Dynasty, spent seven years determining the trigrams' directionality and their proper and present pattern of appearance, shown previously. It was also during the Chou period that associations of greater complexity evolved. For example, the trigram for heaven became connected with heaven in a spiritual sense. This added spiritual dimension established a connection between trigrams and human beings. Gradually the trigrams came to represent the various aspects of human experience. As a record of life experience, the trigrams were depended upon to presage the consequences of any action (good consequences were shown to result from good motives). Because of its immense capacity for bettering human behavior, the trigrams bore great pertinence to human ethics. During the centuries spanning the Fu Hsi and Chou Dynasties, the meaning of the trigrams evolved from a form of pure ontologism to a form of activism to become a rationalism of values. Henceforth, these associations have enduringly provided great practical value for human use. The eight trigrams became the eight guidelines of human attitudes, or Eight Attitudes.

THE TAO OF EIGHT ATTITUDES

☰

I. ATTITUDE OF HEAVEN

The three Yang lines produce an image of absolute progressiveness, the spirit of heaven. (Confucius described heaven as being constantly progressive.) Gentlemen who adopt this spirit never stop improving themselves, thereby gaining an understanding of the true purpose of life. Life is to live: its value is that one will always have something to live for. What one lives for may be called a desire or a dream. In the business world, it is called goals. The basic prerequisite for success, or absolute progressiveness, is the desire to improve oneself.

Such a desire is manifested in the formulation of goals or dreams, which determine the outcome of one's efforts, because it functions as one's direction and driving force. If a burning desire or goal is nonexistent, the drive to do anything is simply not there. That greater goals generate greater achievements is a fact revealed by deeper examination of this image: the three lines may be interpreted (from the bottom up) as immediate goals, mid-range goals, then long-range goals; lowest, higher, and highest goals; or physical, mental, and spiritual goals. These represent just about all the goals known to human experience. We can flip through any page in history and we will never find one successful person who has not set up goals first. But we must also remember the unsuccessful and unknown who have either set wrong goals or none at all.

Experience has shown that goals can be meaningless unless they are written down. Once written down, they become plans. This technique, breaking and writing down your goals in the above context, is extremely powerful when used well.

THE TAO OF EIGHT ATTITUDES

Consider the example set by Konosuke Matsushita of Matsushita Electric Co., who built a nationwide and later multinational corporation from a humble door-to-door merchandising business. Many people, while discussing Japanese management styles, frequently analyze his case and present him as a role model for their theories. Actually the reason for his success is very simple: he is the one who really knows how to adopt this principle. He requires all his managers to submit three types of plans every year: six-month plans, two-year plans, five-year plans, and monthly revisions of these plans. Nothing is overlooked with such a system. Simply put, those who work for him work with a plan or not at all. He is the true essence of someone who practices the aforementioned principles. Can you imagine any individual or organization failing with this kind of attitude?

According to Taoist scholarly teachings, the desire to improve oneself, to form goals, is not an instinct. *True* desire does not originate from within the physical self, but is instead cultivated—that is, deepened and perfected. When that desire has been deepened and perfected to the point that it and the individual has melded together and become inseparable, then it becomes a kind of attitude. For example, Abraham Lincoln and his desire were inseparable; his accomplished goals became so much a part of him that he even died because of them. They became his attitude, which in turn suited him for accomplishing them.

To cultivate a desire, the Sages always suggested that people should begin with deepening and perfecting a desire to make a comfortable living, then progress to deepening and perfecting a desire to contribute to society, and gradually work their way through greater and greater goals, always nurturing each desire until it became a part of them. As Sage Kuei Ku said, "To nurture a dream is a matter straight toward God, with no bending or surrendering. It needs absolute devotion." To summarize, the first attitude concerns goal setting.

The Tao of Eight Attitudes

II. ATTITUDE OF WATER

(This image is different from the seventh trigram, the image of a lake.) This image of oceanic waters connotes purification. As we all know, all forms of life on this planet survive because of the purifying effects of water. And, according to Lao Tzu, the ocean is king of all waters, because all waters under heaven collect there. The image also connotes discipline. Navigation in the ocean is difficult and fraught with unexpected dangers; consequently, sailors must be extremely disciplined in order to remain alive and on course. Discipline allows sailors to be cautious, and caution provides some measure of safety. This principle can be applied with success to navigation through life, which is also fraught with unexpected dangers. That is why Lao Tzu repeatedly encouraged people to learn the wisdom or spirit of water, which to human beings is the spirit of discipline.

Though the meaning of discipline is clear to many, let us look at it another way. The image projected by the trigram (one Yang line interposed between two Yin lines) is that both Yin lines must give in (surrender) to the middle line. Meaning: in order to reach the central goal a person must sacrifice many, many things around him. Just like a person shooting at a target, he must discern and ignore everything that is to the side or away from the target. As Lao Tzu said, "In order to be successful, one must cut off any excessiveness, extravagance, and easy indulgence." Furthermore, if one neglects to purify oneself, one will never even take the first step towards, let alone achieve, one's goal, no matter how grand or noble it is. The importance of discipline cannot be over-stressed.

In general there are five activities that must be disciplined in order for goals to be reached:

A. Contact or involvement with meaningless people.

B. Involvement in useless or meaningless affairs.

C. Thinking too much about nonsensical matters.

D. Excessive amusement or recreation.

E. Talking too much about nonsensical matters.

We are on earth for only a short time: generally speaking, our lives are short. Hence, we must use every available bit of invaluable time efficiently. Supposing for example that our average life span is sixty years, if forty years were spent for childhood, sickness, necessary rest and recreation, old age, and so on, less than twenty years remain for us to accomplish our learning, training, and achievement of goals. Twenty years is 240 months, or about 72,000 days. If we waste one day we die one day for nothing. Most of the people in this world are good people, but they have not achieved anything either. The reason is because they waste away their lives engaged in one or more of the above five activities. They might have been misled into thinking that life was not serious and adopted a nonchalant attitude. Only truly successful people take life seriously.

III. ATTITUDE OF MOUNTAINS

The image is that of a mountain, with one Yang line atop two Yin lines. The image connotes tolerance: all Yin—shortcomings, weaknesses, etc.—have been covered by Yang. The mountain is a mound of earth that is bigger, higher, more abundant than all other mounds of earth. It has an abundance of all species of trees, bushes, animals, gems, springs, rocks, grasses, earth, etc. It does not care whether they are large or small, healthy or diseased, beautiful or ugly. Sage Kuei Ku said, "Why is the mountain grand? Because it does not discriminate against the small trees, small rocks, sand, or even the clay." If one day the mountain tells a kind of shriveled and ugly tree that it does not like it and throws out all of its kind, it will lose a portion of its wealth. If it dislikes a particular kind of earth and throws it out, it will lose a great portion of its size. If it keeps discriminating, it will become as flat and as desolate as the desert. The underlying meaning to this image is this: a lone individual is limited and must need the help of others. Only through the help of others can a person achieve success, so the truly successful person must tolerate other people in order to get their help.

Tolerance is the third attitude of a successful person. The greater the tolerance, the greater the success. When they are upwardly mobile most people can tolerate others for need of their input. But it is after they have achieved their goals that they are really in danger of developing a haughty attitude that causes them to dissociate themselves from those they originally disliked or hesitated to associate with. Then they "burn their bridges," one by one. "When wealth and honors lead to arrogance," as Lao Tzu said, "this brings evil on itself." In another instance, a person who is as hard as a rock and is unreceptive to ideas or advice from others will have a life that leads nowhere. Intolerance of yet another kind, intolerance of a group of people for any reason, may cause one to miss a world of potential help capable of carrying one to greatness. Be aware of the fact that the tolerable few may be completely useless. To help oneself be tolerant, adopt a humble attitude—the key to tolerance. Tolerance is not only enjoyable, but also a most important method of becoming truly wealthy, strong, and grand.

THE TAO OF EIGHT ATTITUDES

IV. ATTITUDE OF THUNDER

Thunder is a stroke of stimulation. Its roar signals the end of winter and the start of spring; subsequently, it has come to symbolize life and creation. Two Yin lines on top and one Yang line on the bottom create an image of the start of something new: new ideas, new timing, etc.

Successful people learn the spirit of thunder, so that they may be constantly creating, always starting anew, always renewing ideas and actions, and always improving. Needless to say this is a golden rule in the corporate world. There must always be new ideas, inventions, improved productions of quality, and so on. But in order to have all this, one must have creative employees. We call this "new blood." Without this injection of new blood, competitiveness is lost, finally resulting in sufferings due to failure.

This is also true on an individual basis. Without creativity, one can neither promote oneself nor hold onto a basic position, as one will no longer be needed. Nobody is designed to come to this world to be fed on a feather bed. In order to survive, many obstacles need to be removed; many bottlenecks, broken through. Without new ideas, new methods, new thinking, new techniques, one will be swept away by a cruel, invisible hand.

In most cases, creativity unfortunately is not one of the instincts, but laziness is. So people need to cultivate creativity until it becomes an attitude; otherwise laziness cannot be overcome.

V. ATTITUDE OF WINDS

Wind is composed of air and pressure. The image of two Yang lines atop one Yin line symbolizes air flowing from areas of high pressure to areas of low pressure. Though the wind is popularly thought to flow of its own free will, this is not so. Air flows from areas of high pressure to areas of low pressure, thus creating the breezes and winds—even the wind has no free will. The spirit of the winds teaches people about the importance of will power. Like the air, human beings live in a world full of pressures; you cannot do anything according to your free will. In order to accomplish anything and ease our own and others' lives we must:

A. Develop an attitude of mercifulness and ease, or kindness, to make our interactions as smooth as the breeze.

B. Develop penetrating concentration skills (the wind squeezes and penetrates through the tiniest cracks).

C. Develop the quality of loyalty (air is always there ready and willing and available to support life, just like a loyal, understanding, wonderful, and powerful friend).

If one lacked any or all of the wind's spirits (one is instead cruel, brusque, selfish, disloyal, etc.) failure is assured. A two-headed viper is always cursed. History is full of examples of such failures who lost everything, including empires, because of these shortcomings. As King Solomon said (Proverb 19:22), "The desire of a man *is* his kindness; and a poor man *is* better than the liar." And as Lao

Tzu said, "Kindness is sure to be victorious even in battle and firmly to defend its ground. One who arms himself with kindness will be protected by Heaven." An attitude of kindness guarantees either victory or protection, regardless of the situation.

VI. ATTITUDE OF FIRE

Fire is like the sun lighting up the day sky and the moon and stars lighting up the night sky. But fire cannot burn by itself. The fire trigram is an image of giving: Yang gives in to Yin, and the Yang lines on both sides of one Yin line in the trigram are giving. Giving is a two-sided affair.

The spirit of fire enlightens human beings to the fact that helping must be mutual. Nobody can survive without another's help. For example, children cannot grow up without parental care. The parents must give unconditionally to care, protect, feed, etc. the baby. Then the baby matures to give his aging parents unconditional care, protection, etc. This kind of loving and caring has been glorified most of the time, but some teachings tilt the scale off-balance by encouraging people to give only and not expect any returns—in other words, accept only and return nothing. The wisdom of fire teaches us that we must have an attitude of returning a favor, any favor. Doing otherwise is to defy the universal principle of balance and encourage severe punishments.

For example, there was a young man who led an absolutely abysmal life, but he was talented and bright—there seemed to be no reason for his failure. The reason was revealed when he complained one day: "All the people who ever gave me anything or helped me in any way always expected something from me in return. They always took back what they gave when I didn't fall for their trick. Their kind of giving is not what I call true giving. True giving is giving without expecting anything in return. So I don't have to do anything to satisfy them. My father once bought me a guitar because he knew I liked music and wanted to play one. But one day, he took it back and scolded me for not playing it or giving it enough care. I hated my father since then because he was not right. He had no right to give me a guitar and expect some kind of behavior in return." His attitude is the cause of all his problems; he completely twisted the principle of giving.

Giving cannot be one-sided. Everyone must give. Returning a favor is another form of the responsibility of giving. To repeat, giving is an important attitude for success. Those who know how to return a favor can receive more help. Those who are unwilling to give in return are absolutely selfish. They use and take advantage of every bit of other people's kindness, but excuse themselves of their responsibilities of contribution. This will naturally result in disaster. The sower expects a harvest, the harvest encourages more sowing.

VII. ATTITUDE OF EARTH

The image of earth is one of silence, retreat, passiveness. Even though the earth is a great supplier, it does so silently. This trigram has three Yin lines, indicating regression.

THE TAO OF EIGHT ATTITUDES

Human life does not go on forever; sooner or later it will reach an end. This is a fact. Nobody should feel sad or regretful, because it cannot be prevented. Instead people should develop an attitude of confronting and dealing with an ending or stopping.

But human nature favors startings and rejects endings, celebrates developings and regrets sustainings.

Why must this be so, when much goodness can be derived from a stop? Sometimes a temporary "stop" in the form of a short vacation in the midst of a busy work schedule can result in better health, sharper minds, happier moods, and better work. Also, some of the best musical compositions have "stops," or pauses, which contribute to its greatness. Moreover, if winter or summer never ended, what would become of this world?

The principle of withdrawal and how one utilizes it can work in favor of one's objectives and constitute a great wisdom. Therefore, cultivating an attitude of withdrawal is beneficial. To illustrate, George Washington resigned from office during the height of his prestige, preserving forevermore his greatness as the father of this country. Immediately, Lao Tzu's words come to mind: "When the work is done, and one's name is becoming distinguished, to withdraw into obscurity is the way of Heaven." If Richard Nixon had followed this principle, only the memory of his success and greatness would have remained in everyone's minds.

One must realize that many situations in this world are not situations of doing or dying. In many cases, an end may only be a beginning (of a legend). The way the lives of Abraham Lincoln, Martin Luther King, and John F. Kennedy ended could have been the most important factor contributing to their eternal fame. A retreat leads to a newer, better, or even historic life.

Unfortunately many teachings advocate a "never-quit" attitude, thereby victimizing many people.

VIII. ATTITUDE OF LAKE

This trigram, with two Yang lines below one Yin line, is an image of an opening in the earth's crust. Filled with water, this opening forms a limited body of water: a lake. Surrounded by mountains, trees, villages, etc., the lake is the very image of joy, peace, and recreation. The spirit of the lake teaches one to rejoice in whatever one toils upon.

Many of the truly successful people in the world all share one same attitude, that of enjoying their work. They need not seek amusement outside their work, because work itself is amusement enough; seeing the work they do benefit humanity is the greatest source of their enjoyment. They need not waste extra time finding entertainment at, for instance, the theater or beaches. In the opposite case, many people hate their work and cannot wait for vacation time or the weekend, which they regard as their only opportunity to find satisfaction in their lives. In order to make sure that their lives are sufficiently fulfilled and that every bit of fun is extracted from precious little time, people get themselves into debt, fight traffic at vacation spots, pay hotel bills, sleep on bad mattresses, eat bad food, get sick, get cramped into crowded jets, suffer jet lag, injure themselves, even lose their jobs (many employers chose vacation times to fire employees) all for "fun." The more people try to sweeten their lives, the more bitter they become.

When a human being evolves, there is a natural desire or force inside him that goads him to climb up. This force is similar to that which pushes a plane off the runway into the air and holds it there. At first a great deal of force or propulsion is needed to push the plane into the air, but once the plane is in the air these forces become maintaining forces (there has to be some force—no rope is holding it up there). If just a bit of that force is lost the plane immediately starts to plummet, and if that force is not recovered the plane will crash. Recreation weakens or cuts off the force that holds us in our precarious evolutionary positions. We know when this force is weakened: we feel relaxed. Recreation, after a long period of hard work, releases the tension and helps people feel refreshed. Coasting is allowed in some situations, but the engines must be started up again to maintain flight. Addiction to physical-level recreation, such as drinking, recreational drugs, sex, etc., shuts down our engines permanently, leaving us to suffer the consequences. "Colour's five hues make people blind; music's five notes make the ears deaf; the five flavours deprive the mouth of taste; the chariot course, and the wild hunting make people's hearts run wild."

Lao Tzu continued, "Heaven and Earth lasts forever, the reason being they serve not their own selfish purposes. This is how they are able to continue and endure. So as the Sages. They put their own personal needs last; therefore, they are preserved." Humanity's interests should be elevated (in another interpretation, the trigram shows an opening for improvement at the top). Interests can be elevated to the mental level through education. For example, Sages cultivate themselves so that they will always place their services to humanity first, always enjoy their responsibilities, and elevate their amusements to the spiritual level, where there is true amusement and rejoicing. Only spiritual level amusements can be truly enjoyed without bad side-effects.

When I was on the board of directors of a Japanese corporation, I noticed something extremely amazing: most of the Japanese corporations not only adopted some or all of the above eight attitudinal principles as teaching guidelines and mottos, but also systemized them so that they were a part of the corporate function. Matsushita

THE TAO OF EIGHT ATTITUDES

Electric Co. is only one well-known example; the eight principles can be found more or less intact in every Japanese organization. The systemizing of the principles actually began with Iyeyasu Tokugawa (1542-1616 A.D.). The principles, adopted even earlier for use in many aspects of Japanese life, were also used as domestic regulations; and the Tokugawas first began with systemizing these. So today the Japanese corporations have a system for training, disciplining . . . even stress training their managers. The corporations also acclimitize their managers to change and teach them the handling of change. The corporations shape their managers into right people (prepared individuals). Such a situation cannot be found anywhere else in the world. Their systemization of these Eight Attitudes was *the* secret that allowed their accomplishments to reverberate throughout the world. Little wonder why their competitiveness is unmatched.

In ancient China the responsibility of cultivating these attitudes and scholastic skills in children rested with the family. Every honorable family had its own laws, or course of emphasis, because the inculcation of these attitudes in children was taken very seriously. If a member of the family failed in society because of an attitude problem, the entire family including the ancestors were disgraced. Later on, when advanced learning was sought, students could depend on the mentor-protege system of education to complete their training. To the protege, the mentor was a teacher, parent, superior, and friend. Such training provided Chinese history with countless examples of heroism.

Japan also incorporated the mentor-protege system of education into their higher-level educational and corporate systems. When I was doing graduate research in a Japanese university, I found that the mentor-protege system had been emphasized to a point that was unimaginable. Upon leaving school, the Japanese who is hired by a corporation enters into another mentor-protege system, one that is devised by the corporation to forge a superior-subordinate bond that far exceeds conventional employer-employee bonds. The superior becomes a teacher, father, and friend. Under these conditions teamwork arises automatically—another factor in Japanese competitive power.

The application of the Eight Attitudes guarantees that a cultivator's personality will be enriched, so that he may become a right person.

So will the study of the Eight Blessings. It is amazing how the Eight Blessings of Jesus (Matthew 5:3-10) are similar to the Eight Attitudes:

> Blessed *are* the poor in spirit: for theirs is the kingdom of heaven. Blessed *are* they that mourn: for they shall be comforted. Blessed *are* the meek: for they shall inherit the earth. Blessed *are* they which do hunger and thirst after righteousness: for they shall be filled. Blessed *are* the merciful: for they shall obtain mercy. Blessed *are* the pure in heart: for they shall see God. Blessed *are* the peacemakers: for they shall be called the children of God. Blessed *are* they which *are* persecuted for righteousness' sake: for theirs is the kingdom of heaven.

Each of the eight trigrams has been shown earlier to have directionality. Applying the directions to the Eight Attitudes gives rise to the Directionology for Mental Attitudes, which provides a method for impressing the attitudes into the subconscious. If you feel you have a weakness of a particular attitude, you may face its corresponding direction and contemplate on the various aspects of that attitude. Physically moving your body helps focus your attention on that attitude.

There are also eight simple Internal Exercises to help. (These exercises strengthen the internal organs, which are critical to physical and mental prowess.) It has been recommended that these exercises be done five minutes a day to enrich or strengthen these attitudes.

NORTHWEST

≡

For the Northwestern Exercise, have the front of the body face northwest. Stand with the feet shoulder-width apart. Point the toes inward, so that the feet form an inverted V. This takes the pressure off the nerve endings in your heels and prevents imbalance in pressure.

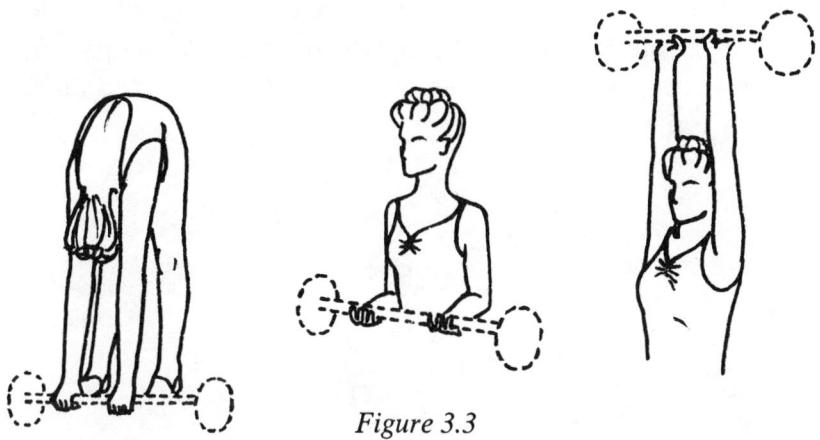

Figure 3.3

Now pretend you are lifting a barbell of medium weight (to prevent too much straining). While keeping the legs straight, bend down to pick up an imaginary barbell. Lift the barbell to waist level. Then lift the barbell as high as possible above your head. Visualize that you are actually lifting a barbell. Then reverse this procedure. Do the exercise as many times as you want.

This exercise helps increase your strength. It is also good for your lungs and large intestines, as well as your attitude.

NORTH

▬▬ ▬▬
▬▬▬▬▬
▬▬ ▬▬

For the Northern Exercise, direct the front of your body to the north. Spread the feet wide apart and bend your knees. Ideally your thighs should form a straight line, but if this position is uncomfortable for any amount of time, readjust the bend to your comfort level. Hold the torso straight, not tilted forward or backward. Now pretend you are shooting an arrow from a bow. Shoot to your right and to your left. Your head, arms, and torso change positions, but your feet and legs remain stationary. Really visualize that you are pulling a taut bowstring and shooting an arrow. Do this exercise as many times as you wish.

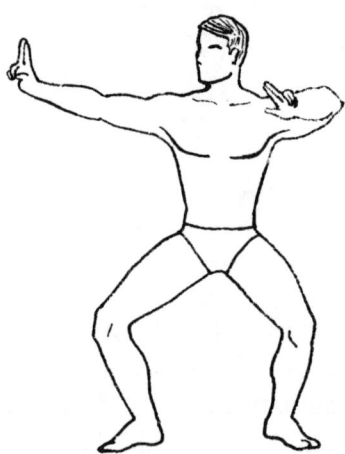

Figure 3.4

This exercise is also good for the lungs, kidneys, large intestines, bladder, skin, and bones.

NORTHEAST

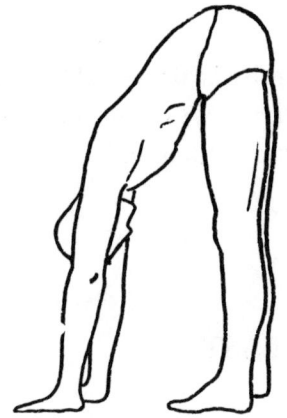

Facing northeast, bend down and touch the toes with your fingertips. Keep the legs straight. Bend as much as possible; if you can place your hands on the floor, do so. Then visualize a mountain. You may hold this position as long as you wish.

This exercise is also good for the spleen-pancreas, muscle, and digestion.

Figure 3.5

EAST

In the morning, stand in the sunlight and have the front of your body face east. Place your feet shoulder-width apart. Point the toes inward and close your eyes. With your arms hanging at your sides, turn the upper body to the sides. Let your head turn with the torso. Let the eyes trace the source of radiant heat emitted by the sun. Do not move the lower half of the body. As you turn from side to side

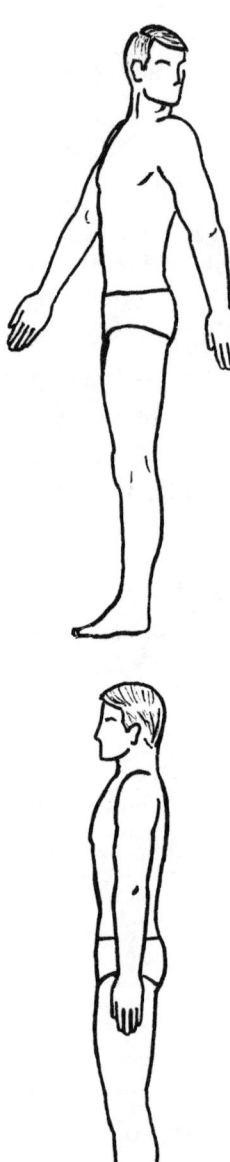

in a steady and smooth motion, your mind should be following these movements—never let it wander. Do this as long as you like.

This exercise is also good for the nerves, liver, eyes, gall bladder, and weight reduction.

Figure 3.6

SOUTHEAST

Facing southeast, stand with your feet shoulder-width apart. Point your toes inward and raise yourself on your toes. Lower yourself. The upper body should be kept straight. Do this seven times as a set. If you wish, you may do more. Do not let your mind wander.

This exercise also benefits the nerves, liver, gall bladder, and heart.

Figure 3.7

The Tao of Eight Attitudes

Figure 3.8

SOUTH

Facing south, rotate your hips as if you had a hoola-hoop around you. You may reverse the direction of the rotation as you wish. Never let your mind wander. Do this exercise for as long as you wish.

This exercise is also good for the sexual organs.

SOUTHWEST

Figure 3.9

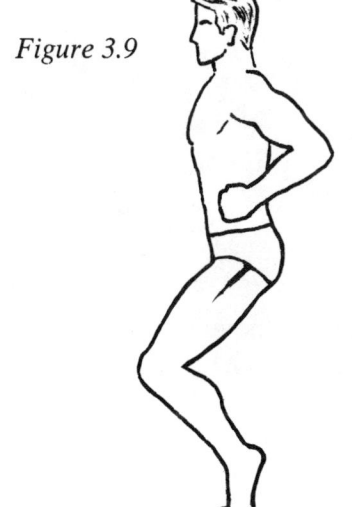

Facing southwest, pose as if you were about to fight. Bend the knees slightly. Bend the arms slightly and clench the fists. Make your eyes bulge out as if in a rage. Your mind must be with your body. Hold this pose as long as you wish.

This exercise also benefits the digestive system, lungs, and nerves.

THE TAO OF EIGHT ATTITUDES

WEST

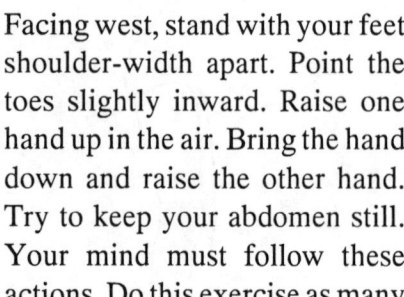

Facing west, stand with your feet shoulder-width apart. Point the toes slightly inward. Raise one hand up in the air. Bring the hand down and raise the other hand. Try to keep your abdomen still. Your mind must follow these actions. Do this exercise as many times as you wish.

This exercise also benefits lower back pain, shoulder pain, kidney problems, and spinal problems.

Figure 3.10

These exercises can be done anywhere, anytime. In two minutes, anyone can energize their bodies and minds. Then business or other problems can be solved easily.

CHAPTER 4

THE TAO OF POSITIONING

After becoming fully trained and prepared, one must seek proper positions so that growth may continue and abilities may be proven. According to Sage Kuei Ku there are five groups of possible factors bringing individuals and positions together:

1) Moral standard, valuable issues, inventions, ingenuity, reputation. . . .

2) Parties, associations, teams, communities. . . .

3) Benefit, profit, assistance, competition. . . .

4) Sexual relations, favor collection, trade, coercion. . . .

5) Heritage, mentor-protege associations. . . .

The Tao of Positioning

A position is a territory within which you will carry out your mission and confirm your ability to perform, negotiate, organize, and delegate responsibilities. Specifically, it is where you complete a project on time and within budget, motivate staff, resolve conflicts, solve endless problems, make endless decisions, control product quality and services, please superiors, and preserve your position, which may be eagerly awaited by others. And of course, position is also a source of reward (the side of the coin emphasized most), such as power, money, status, or fame.

No matter what position you have in mind, or what enables you to get a position, a position is best secured or guaranteed by being needed.

How do you ensure your matchlessness? The Sage pointed out six strategies:

1) When the organization or superior is in some kind of trouble, confusion, or difficulty, you are the one who is able to discern and analyze the root of the problems and put forth the best solution to correct them.

2) New ideas or inventions are always coming out, but you are the one who understands and helps their creators be recognized.

3) A theory or solution that can provide tremendous results in one or many areas lies unexercised, but you are the one who discovers it and makes it available.

4) A situation or matter of great potential is dangling in uncertainty, but you are the one who is able to settle it.

5) Many unwanted problems spring up, but you are the one who is able to minimize the risk or damage.

6) When disaster comes, you are the one who stands up and

The Tao of Positioning

confronts it, putting the organization or superior under your protection.

If you believe your talent, training, and personality enable you to be constructive and capable, you will always be needed—perhaps even be honored. Positions, promotions, and perhaps awards await you. "As long as the net is available, the beast will fall in. As long as the bait is there, fish will come," guaranteed the Sage.

In the past twenty years many people at many different positions in life and work have sought my counsel. To each and everyone of them I gave advice in accordance with the above six principles; and I am delighted to report that the success rate proved to be higher than eighty percent. Because of the aforementioned teachings, many people have become useful, and many useful people have become great. Once the truth was accepted, practicing these strategies enabled everybody to win.

But a small percentage, even if they applied everything they learned, still did not get a decent promotion. One might say the employers must have been blind. Yes, sometimes they were "blind." At least, they were blocked. No matter what people did their employers just did not see their worth. Or when the employers finally opened their eyes and were just about to promote, someone unworthy but one step ahead snatched away that chance. If I only told you the positive side—*You do this or that and you'll be okay*—I would be lying, and hence also the Sage. Whoever offers that kind of statement offers only temporary stimulation. To be realistic Sage Kuei Ku pointed out situations that might block your advance (unfortunately, these situations existed from the beginning in any organization or region in the world):

1) Some co-workers are good people but just too sensitive. In trying to overcome their extremely insecure feelings, they anxiously use all kinds of normal or abnormal approaches to get ahead.

The Tao of Positioning

2) Some co-workers suddenly become very greedy for material needs or other attractions and turn around and sell you out.

3) Some co-workers feel they have lost all hope. They may try something to pull you back, just to make themselves feel a little better.

4) Some have special relationships, including those of sex, blood, blackmail, etc., so their promotion will be considered preferentially.

5) The way up is simply too crowded. There are too many people ahead of you awaiting promotions. And there is absolutely no way to step in or step up.

6) The organization is extremely unorganized or in a very bad situation, so there is little or no chance of a promotion. The priority is survival, not promotion.

If one of the above situations exist, your position or future is in great jeopardy. Sometimes you might not be able to correct it. In these situations most people will be stressed, feel depressed, become ill, or behave foolishly by resorting to self-destructive acts. To safeguard sanity and lives, Sage Kuei Ku and other ancient Sages gave four ways of combatting such situations.

1) Leave for good. The Sage said, "Retreat is the top strategy. Even a worm or insect knows about using withdrawal or escape to protect itself."

   a) Remove yourself from the situation temporarily. That way you will be able to have a clear mind to analyze, think, and plan, because there is always a life ahead.

The Tao of Positioning

b) There isn't a permanent situation in the world. Perhaps a new position or opportunity needs you to seek it out. The old situation is just something that pushes you to seek better alternatives. Sometimes, a good person needs to be pushed by evil, because good people would rather remain stationary.

c) A wise man only goes to places where he is supposed to be. He should avoid being in wrong places in the first place, because once he sets foot in a wrong place he loses chances of getting to a right place.

2) The Sage said that man must know his time. Nobody can fight time. Only the knowledge of it reveals the right time in which something may or may not be done. If time is on your side, you are riding a sun chariot straight up. In the opposite case you cannot do anything but wait and be patient. Your chance will come again as time is cyclical.

3) Universal will. Mencius, the scholar second only to Confucius, said, "Heaven chooses a person who shall bear great responsibility. First let him experience hard labor, starvation, poverty, heartbreak, deep distress, all kinds of adversity. Then his true capability shall be increased." Similarly, Lao Tzu advised, "Hero, conquer not the world, before conquering thyself first."

4) Universal procedure. There are three steps which lead to great leadership. Lao Tzu named them as follows:

Yu-wei,
Wu-wei,
Wu-pu-wei

The Tao of Positioning

Meaning: "Do," "Doing nothing," and "Everything can be done." Every great person must pass through these three steps of life. The first step is preparation; the second, adversity; the third, service and mission accomplishment. (Recall the life of Chiang, Shang.)

The life of Moses is another exemplification of these rules. His entire life, 120 years, was clearly divided into three periods, as described in Acts 7:20-36:

> In which time Moses was born, and was exceeding fair, and nourished up in his father's house three months:
>
> And when he was cast out, Pharaoh's daughter took him up, and nourished him for her own son.
>
> And Moses was learned in all the wisdom of the Egyptians, and was mighty in words and in deeds.
>
> And when he was full <u>forty years old</u>, it came into his heart to visit his brethren the children of Israel.
>
> And seeing one *of them* suffer wrong, he defended *him*, and avenged him that was oppressed, and smote the Egyptian:
>
> For he supposed his brethren would have understood how that God by his hand would deliver them: but they understood not.
>
> And the next day he shewed himself unto them as they strove, and would have set them at one again, saying, Sirs, ye are brethren; why do ye wrong one to another?

The Tao of Positioning

But he that did his neighbour wrong thrust him away, saying, Who made thee a ruler and a judge over us?

Wilt thou kill me, as thou didest the Egyptian yesterday?

Then fled Moses at this saying, and was a stranger in the land of Madian, where he begat two sons.

And when <u>forty years</u> were expired, there appeared to him in the wilderness of mount Sina an angel of the Lord in a flame of fire in a bush.

. . . .

This Moses whom they refused, saying, Who made thee a ruler and a judge? the same did God send *to be* a ruler and a deliverer by the hand of the angel which appeared to him in the bush.

He brought them out, after that he had shewed wonders and signs in the land of Egypt, and in the Red sea, and in the wilderness <u>forty years</u>.

CHAPTER 5

THE TAO OF FIVE-STAR SYSTEM

Besides becoming a right person and acquiring a right position, a person must deal with the right people. In dealing with people, it is best to know them first. Truly knowing people is the most difficult matter in the world for managers or anybody else in any situation.

In order to help us know people thoroughly, accurately, clearly, and quickly, the ancient Taoist scholars provided us with a formula. But before we can utilize this formula we must look at another application of the Yin-Yang theories. It is quite amazing that the ancients had perfect knowledge of the so-called "new study of the modern age"—the study of the human brain and its newly formulated theories. What is even more amazing is that the ancients had the ability to utilize the knowledge for practical use. As we may already know, modern studies show the human brain to be divided into two hemispheres: the right and left. The left hemisphere dominates the right side of the body and is the basis for an analytical, critical, logical personality. The right hemisphere dominates the left side of the body and gives the human being an artistic, philosophical, political personality. Millenniums ago, when he wrote the *Classics of the Internal* (*Nei Ching* and *Ling-Su Ching*), the Yellow Emperor divided the brain into Yin and Yang sides, according to their properties. Furthermore, he classified people's personalities by the dominant sides of their brains. A Yin Personality is exactly like the personality with a dominant left brain, and a Yang Personality is exactly like that with a dominant right brain. The first of two big differences between the ancient and modern studies is that a *third* type of personality—one that has qualities contributed by both halves of the brain—has been pointed out by the Yellow Emperor. Such personalities, because of their thought and active processes, are classified as the Balanced Yin-Yang Personalities. The second difference is that divisions within the hemispheres themselves have been found by the Yellow Emperor. So those who are dominated by the lower and upper halves of the left brain are called, respectively, Lesser Yin and Greater Yin Personalities. And those who are dominated by the lower and upper halves of the right brain are called, respectively, Lesser Yang and Greater Yang Personalities.

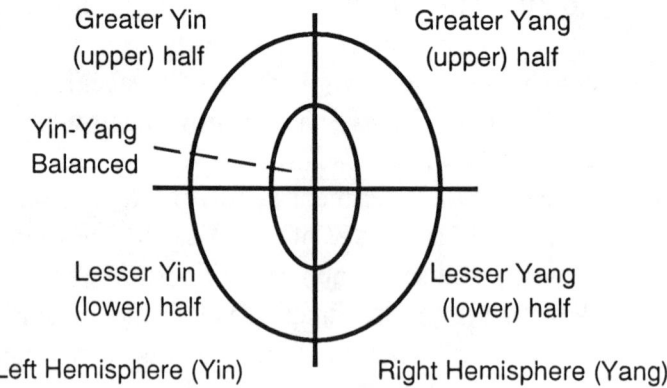

Figure 5.1 Divisions of the Brain

THE TAO OF FIVE-STAR SYSTEM

In total there are five major types of personalities, consistent with the numerical basis for the Taoist Theory of Five Elements (to be explained next). The only modern equivalents of these five personalities—called Five Yin-Yang Personalities—may be the Type A and Type B Personalities.

These five personalities serve as the basis for a system, called Five-Star System, that reveals the inner workings of an individual, makes the five personalities function harmoniously and efficiently together, cancels out each personality's bad traits, and stimulates and generates each personality's good traits. How this simple system magnifies managerial effectiveness will be explained in the paragraphs that follow. But before we delve into the details, there must first be an understanding of the Five-Element Theory.

The ancient Taoist scholars, by observing and contemplating the workings of the universe, devised a theory to explain the balance of the complimentary and antagonistic units of which it is composed. The characteristics and relationships of these dynamic units are explained in the Theory of Five Elements.

In this theory, the life force in all of its myriad manifestations comes into and goes out of existence through the interplay of the Five Elements: Fire, Earth, Metal, Water, and Wood. This five-element model is unique to Taoism, because ancient Western and Indian philosophy used a four-element model, which consists of the elements Earth, Air, Water, and Fire. In Taoism, Air is included in the concept of Fire, for without air, fire would not burn.

There are two cycles that illustrate the interaction between these elements. In the Yang Cycle—the cycle of generation—each element generates or produces the succeeding element: thus wood generates fire, fire generates earth, earth produces metal, metal generates liquids (water), water generates wood—the cycle begins again. In the Yin Cycle—the cycle of destruction—each element destroys or absorbs the succeeding element: thus fire liquefies and destroys metal, metal cleaves and destroys wood, wood absorbs earth, earth absorbs water, water absorbs fire, fire destroys metal—the cycle begins again.

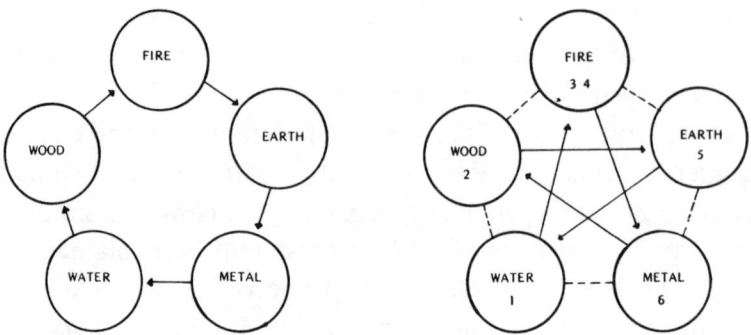

Figure 5.2 Cycle of Generation   Figure 5.3 Cycle of Destruction

Because the universe maintains balance through the interplay of the Five Elements in Yin-Yang Cycles, our bodies, as microcosms of the universe, are thought to achieve mental and physical harmony in the same way. Energy flows through the body via the meridians and their respective organs and bowels in well-defined cycles. The cycles depicting the flow of energy within the body mirror the two cycles that depict the interaction between the five elements. Taoism identifies each of the viscera with one of the elements in the following manner:

```
fire—heart                    metal—lungs
      small intestine               large intestine
      triple heater                 skin
        (endocrine glands)  water—kidneys
      heart constrictor             bladder
                                    bones
earth—spleen-pancreas         wood—liver
      stomach                       gallbladder
      muscle                        nerves
```

The Tao of Five-Star System

The elements as assigned to the Organs and Bowels are:

Table 5.1

	Wood	Fire (Prince)	Earth	Metal	Water	Fire (Minister)
Organ	Liver	Heart	Spleen	Lungs	Kidneys	Heart Constrictor
Bowel	Gall-bladder	Small Intestine	Stomach	Large Intestine	Bladder	Triple Heater

Identifying each of the organs with its respective element in the first cycle results in: the heart (fire) supporting the spleen-pancreas (earth); the spleen-pancreas (earth), the lungs (metal); the lungs (metal), the kidneys (water); the kidneys (water), the liver (wood); the liver (wood), the heart (fire). The bowels also follow the same cycle: the small intestine (fire) supports the stomach (earth); the stomach (earth), the large intestine (metal); the large intestine (metal), the bladder (water); the bladder (water), the gallbladder (wood).

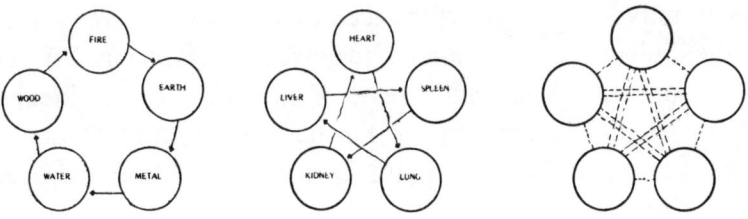

Figure 5.4

If the energy within an organ is not balanced, that organ, rather than being able to effectively support the organ succeeding it on the meridian circuit, will adversely affect, or will be adversely affected by, another organ. This pattern has been depicted in the second cycle of the interaction between the elements in which each element destroys or absorbs the other. Thus, when the energy within the heart (fire) is imbalanced, it (heart, fire) will adversely affect the lungs (metal); the lungs (metal), the liver (wood); the liver (wood), the spleen-pancreas (earth); the spleen-pancreas (earth), the kidneys (water); the kidneys (water), the heart (fire). The second also applies to the bowels: imbalanced energy within the small intestine (fire) will cause it to adversely affect the large intestine (metal); the large intestine (metal), the gallbladder (wood); the gallbladder (wood), the stomach (earth); the stomach (earth), the bladder (water); the bladder (water), the small intestine (fire).

In showing that the cyclic interaction between the organs and bowels is identical to the interaction between the elements, the Taoist scholars provided a means by which the sayings, "That which is above is the same as that which is below" and "The microcosm reflects the macrocosm," could be realized and understood. They also provided a means whereby the interaction of energy between the organs and bowels could be accepted as fact. The basis for that interaction is founded upon the very same logic whereby the interaction of the five elements is instinctively realized to be true.

Likewise, the human brain is a microcosm of the entire body, and thus the universe. It too works in accordance with the Five Elements. All the divisions of the brain—Greater Yin, Lesser Yin, Yin-Yang Balanced, Lesser Yang, and Greater Yang—may then be identified with an element thus: Greater Yin becomes Water; Lesser Yin, Metal; Yin-Yang Balanced, Earth; Lesser Yang, Wood; and Greater Yang, Fire.

Subsequently, each of the Five Yin-Yang Personalities may be renamed thus: Greater Yin Personality becomes a Water Personality; Lesser Yin Personality, Metal Personality; Yin-Yang Balanced Personality, Earth Personality; Lesser Yang Personality, Wood Personality; and Greater Yang Personality, Fire Personality. This gives us the Five-Element Personalities.

THE TAO OF FIVE-STAR SYSTEM

The balance maintained through the interplay of the Five-Element Personalities serves as the basis of the Five-Star System.

Now we shall begin discussing the Five-Star System by describing the principle players—the Five-Element Personalities.

PERSONALITY TYPE: WATER

Figure 5.5

A. Appearance:

Head relatively big. Chin pointed. Face uneven. Complexion dull or dim. Relatively small and narrow shoulder. Thick waist. Hands and feet moving smoothly. Upper and lower back long. Water retentive tissues. Soft and fleshy. Sweats easily and profusely. Clean. Body swings when walking.

B. Behavior:

Superficially calm and easy-going. Seemingly humble and polite. Diplomatic. Creative, flexible, and unstable. Loves change. Self-sacrificing. Emotional. Untrusting and suspicious. Affected. Lacks self-confidence, yet self-assertive. Aloof. Insecure and dependent. Unadventurous and timid. Fearful of storms, heights, earthquakes, floods, and other disasters. Self-abusive. Pessimistic. Irritable.

C. Language (Body and Verbal):

Pretends to listen carefully. Carefully notes words and feedbacks. Smooth talking. Leaves things unsaid. Diverges from topic of discussion. Self-contradictory. Loves to tease and insult. Seldomly praises others. Uses extremely mean words when angry.

D. Interests:

Salty, spicy foods (does not care too much for sweets). Dim lights. Cleanness. Calming environments. Detective stories. Puzzle solving. Chess and other games. Weaponry. Dark or white colors. Uncomfortable with yellow.

E. Health Condition:

Eye problems, dry tongue, sore throat, neck pain, headaches, dull chest pain, palpitation, loose bowels, lumbago, lack of sexual drive, menstrual difficulties, problems with urination, kidney or bladder infections, hemorrhoids. Lack of strength in legs. Hot, tired, painful feet. Poor circulation. Blood pressure and blood sugar problems. Tiredness. Troubled sleep. Water retention.

F. General Description:

Not straightforward, informal, irregular, spineless, easy-going yet complaining.

G. Combinative Effects:

When the parts of the brain designated below are found to be especially prominent, the resulting effects are listed by the Yellow Emperor:

1. Water/Fire (dominant upper left and right brain sections): Calm, gloomy.

2. Water/Wood (dominant upper left and lower right brain sections): Sneaky, accommodating.

3. Water/Water (doubly dominant upper left brain): Very selfish, spineless, and scheming.

4. Water/Metal (dominant upper left and lower left brain sections): Immaculate.

PERSONALITY TYPE: METAL

Figure 5.6

A. Appearance:

Square face. Bright complexion. Head relatively small. Square shoulder. Thin waist. Hands and feet relatively small. Light bones. Clean.

B. Behavior:

Trusting after doubting. Hasty, superior, fierce, loyal, magnanimous, vainglorious, sharp-minded—always the knight-errant. Obedient. Sensitive, compassionate, and amorous. Progressive, determinate, expansive, extravagant. Exaggerating. Has a driving need for recognition and approval and often blames others to cover up faults. Shallow. Contrary and stubborn. Greedy. Judgemental. Secretive. Easily changes focus.

C. Language (Body and Verbal):

Authoritative, directing, demonstrative. Hypothetical, theoretical. Humorous and joking. Boasting. Narrative. Opinionated and comparative. Empty and meaningless. Jumps to conclusions.

D. Interests:

Spicy and sweet foods (does not care for bitter foods). Bright, light, golden colors. Uncomfortable in red. Cleanliness. Sports, martial skill, military science. Romance. Beautiful or expensive things. Accepting gifts. Movable objects (electronic gadgetry, etc.). Clothing. Art.

E. Health Conditions:

Skin problems, gum disease, coughing, allergies, neck and thyroid problems, shoulder pain, arm and back pain, tuberculosis, asthma, pneumonia, stomach pain, colitis, diarrhea, wet dream. Insomnia, fever, sadness, emotional stress. Dreads cold.

F. General Description:

Boasting, compassionate, stubborn, and loyal.

G. Combinative Effects:

1. Metal/Fire (dominant lower left and upper right brain sections): Detailed, calculating.

2. Metal/Wood (dominant lower right and lower left brain sections): Restricted, secretive.

3. Metal/Water (dominant lower and upper left brain sections): Clean, neat.

4. Metal/Metal (doubly dominant lower left brain): Elegant, dashing.

PERSONALITY TYPE: FIRE

Figure 5.7

A. Appearance:

Relatively small headed. Bony, skinny face. Florid complexion. Broad shoulders. Hands and feet correctly sized. Body structure balanced. Light and steady walk. Shoulder swings when walking.

B. Behavior:

Determined, zealous, and fanatical. Always fighting for a cause. Quick, clever, and smooth. Optimistic and positive. Meticulous. Intuitive, changes thoughts. Powerfully desirous. Impatient, unrestrained, bursting, risky, impulsive. Shrewd. Doubts after trusting. Tyrannical.

C. Language (Body and Verbal):

Straightforward, not analytical. Excited and exaggerated. Confident, commanding, friendly, open, freely expressive, unpremeditated. Interrupts others in mid-conversation. Fast speech. Yells when angry.

D. Interests:

Coping with emergencies, assuming responsibilities, fast-lane lifestyle, and playing group sports or games. Sour and bitter tasting foods (does not care for salty foods). Loves beauty, spending, or expensive things. Red, blue, green colors. Uncomfortable in black or dark colors.

E. Health Condition:

Sore eyes, ringing in ears, dry tongue and mouth, burning face, brain diseases, inner arm pain, back and shoulder pain, chest pain, palpitation, heart attacks, strokes, indigestion, weak thighs. High blood pressure, irregular pulse, hot and cold flashes, over-excitement.

F. General Description:

Sensational, abundant common sense, active, driving.

G. Combinative Effects:

1. Fire/Fire (doubly dominant upper right brain): Very impulsive.

2. Fire/Wood (dominant upper and lower right brain sections): Optimistic.

3. Fire/Water (dominant upper right and left brain sections): Superficial, vulgar.

4. Fire/Metal (dominant upper right and lower left brain sections): Humble, pleasant, contented.

PERSONALITY TYPE: WOOD

Figure 5.8

A. Appearance:

Complexion having a pale or bluish cast. Small or long face. Shoulder relatively strong. Back straight. Body slim. Hands and feet thin. Agile hands. Weak constitution.

B. Behavior:

Rational. Persistent, enduring, and hardworking. Independent. Indignant. Strong goals, careful, reserved, well-scheduled. Imaginative. Easily confused, self-doubting, dissatisfied, ambiguous, skeptical, doubting. Egotistical, biased, oppressive, forceful, uncompassionate. Monotonous, depressed, worried, tense, stressed, illusional, reclusive, eccentric.

C. Language (Body and Verbal):

Smiling when listening. Nervous. Hesitant speech, thinking while talking. Pedantic, inconclusive, and ambiguous. Talks at great length (more than necessary). Theoretical. Well-educated and well-studied. Distorted views. Unvarying. Doubting.

D. Interests:

Sour and salty foods (does not care for spicy foods). Blue, dark colors. Not comfortable with white or light colors. Research, thinking, working, and regulating. Criticizing. Excursions, music, swimming, fishing.

E. Health Condition:

Eyesight problems. Eyeball yellowish. Bitter taste in

mouth, headache, migraine, chest pressure, heartburn, back pain, stomach pain, liver problems, gallbladder problems, hernia, vomiting, abnormal stools, testicle pain, menstrual difficulties. Inability to think straight. Depression. Arthritis. Susceptible to tumors.

F. General Description:

Haughty, prejudiced, creative, careful.

G. Combinative Effects:

1. Wood/Fire (dominant lower and upper right brain sections): Pushy, aggressive.

2. Wood/Wood (doubly dominant lower right brain): Obedient, harmonious.

3. Wood/Water (dominant lower right and upper left brain sections): Indignant, unsatisfied.

4. Wood/Metal (dominant lower right and lower left brain sections): Isolated, synthesizing.

PERSONALITY TYPE: EARTH

Figure 5.9

A. Appearance:

Sallow complexion. Round face. Relatively large head. Solid, meaty shoulder. Tendency towards big bellies. Meaty, firm, and strong limbs. Upper and lower body even. Stable walk. Firm steps.

B. Behavior:

Tolerant, mediating, avoids arguments, harmonious, cooperative, self-controlled, ingratiating, quiet, patient. Practical, organized, responsible, coordinating. Economical. Enduring. Lukewarm and repressed. Self-centered. Competitive. Plodding. Profit or benefit oriented.

C. Language (Body and Verbal):

Smoothly communicative. Boasting for practical purposes. Unopinionated. Praises others so that everyone is happy. Likes gossip.

D. Interests:

Sweets. Does not care for sour or spicy foods. Neutrality (dislikes fighting and does not care for sports).

E. Health Condition:

Lightheadedness, heart problems, stomachache, indigestion and other stomach problems, pancreas problems, diabetes, hypoglycemia, eliminatory problems, flatulence. Overweight. Fatigued. Over-worrying. Light sleep. Cold.

F. General Description:

Cautious, generous, gentle.

G. Combinative Effects:

1. Earth/Fire (dominant central and upper right brain sections): Crafty, good to everybody.

2. Earth/Wood (dominant central and lower right brain sections): Dissastisfied, suffering, hardworking.

3. Earth/Water (dominant central and upper left brain sections): Serious, sober, symmetrical.

4. Earth/Metal (dominant central and lower left brain sections): At ease, peaceful, forgiving.

All told there are twenty-five types of personalities. Identifying them does not come easily, according to the Yellow Emperor; that ability is acquired only after long and careful observation and practice. Carefully check each individual's appearance, behavior, body and verbal languages, interests, and health condition, taking as much time as necessary to prove each case. The effort spent is sure to pay off thousandfold.

In case you need to do a quick identification, it is suggested by the Yellow Emperor that you first distinguish Greater and Lesser Yin Personalities from Greater and Lesser Yang or Yin-Yang Balanced Personalities by these clues: Yang personalities like to thrust forward their chests or stomachs; Yin personalities always bend forward at the neck or chest, caving in their chests. The more extreme the posture, the stronger the suggestion of either a Greater Yin or Greater Yang personality. Yin-Yang personalities are balanced. From these simple identifications, you can then immediately recall the distinguishing characteristics of each personality.

Knowledge of personalities is of utmost importance in the working environment. If a manager assigns a "wrong person" to work on a "wrong job," everything will go wrong.

How do you match the "right" person to the "right" job? The Five-Star System provides a very simple formula: the Water Personality should work on Water-style jobs; Wood Personality, Wood-style jobs; Metal Personality, Metal-style jobs; Fire Personality, Fire-style jobs; Earth Personality, Earth-style jobs. A proper match assures highest results and highest satisfaction automatically.

Since jobs have distinct personalities, they can be categorized under the five elements as follows:

1) Water: Jobs related to finance, accounting, book-keeping, bank operation.

2) Metal: Jobs related to law enforcement or interpretation (police, detective, judges, lawyers, etc.), espionage, acting, controls (investigation, inspection, impeachment).

3) Earth: Jobs related to commerce, administration, production, services.

4) Fire: Jobs related to administration, warfare, exploration, intense sports.

5) Wood: Jobs related to planning, research, invention, staffing.

There are many jobs that straddle the elemental boundaries. So all twenty-five types of personalities can be properly matched at the manager's wise discretion.

But to achieve harmony and efficiency—balance—among the members of an organization, just matching the "right person" to the "right job" is not enough. We must delve deeper into the Five-Star System.

THE TAO OF FIVE-STAR SYSTEM

The Five-Element Theory is the means by which cells, tissues, organs, organ-systems, individuals, populations, ecosystems, the biosphere, and the universe attain balance. It is only in a state of balance that life processes will function and continue. One need only recall how the cycle of destruction unleashed by chemicals in the environment inevitably envelops all life forms to understand the seriousness and delicateness of this balance. The balance of an organization is no less delicate. If it is disturbed in any way, the organization is in danger of dying. It is precisely to maintain balance among an organization's vital human constituents that they are categorized into five major personalities, that the Yin-Yang Cycles of the Five-Element Theory are brought to bear upon human interactions, so that an organization may have an instrument to research and complete its balance.

Most of us are all too familiar with the condition of imbalance. For example, if someone fitting the description of the Fire Personality must work alongside someone fitting the description of the Water Personality, these two will have a very hard time getting along with each other. No matter how one tries to resolve personnel conflicts like theirs through education, motivation, or threats, conflicts will continue. Left without alternatives, the structure of the organization is blamed. Restructuring an entire organization because of such conflicts offers no guarantees of better results and is economically unfeasible. The wisest solution would be to place a Wood Personality to work with them, and a seemingly endless problem would be solved immediately.

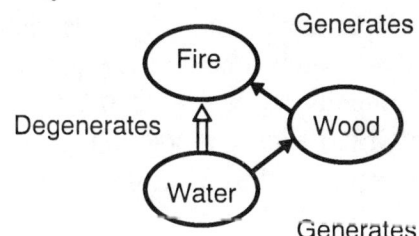

Figure 5.10

The Tao of Five-Star System

I have seen countless cases where corporate personnel conflicts generated tremendous headaches. They are some of the most difficult problems faced by anyone. I have also seen countless cases where such problems were solved with incredible ease by a simple diagnostic procedure and a simple personnel adjustment.

At the next level, the Five-Star System may be applied to the divisions within an organization.

Any organization or its functions may be broken down into what are called Five-Element Departments or Five-Element Functions to reach a complete balance to generate the highest performance and the most satisfactory levels of productivity. The five departments or functions, in the corporate case, are as follows:

Table 5.2

1	2	3	4	5
Wood	Fire	Earth	Metal	Water
Planning Invention Legislature	Administration Personnel	Production Service	Controller Judiciary	General accounting Treasury

These Five-Element Departments or Functions also interact with and balance one another in accordance with the Yin-Yang Cycles. Ideally the department should be further quinque-sected, so that a total of twenty-five sub-functions result. Quinque-section of departments into subunits according to the five-element model encourages a natural, balanced interaction among departmental subunits. This produces an entire department that functions as close to perfection as possible. When near-perfect departments come together to form a balanced organization, one can be sure the organization will be the most perfect existing, operating in the most efficient and economic way possible. Lao Tzu suggested that organizations be kept small in size, in order to enhance the results. A big dinosaur is only doomed for extinction.

The Five-Element Functions need not be clearly confined to five departments as long as the five functions are perfectly balanced. For example, the U.S. government is divided into three departments: legislative, executive, and judicial branches. But in reality the legislative branch absorbs some functions of a fourth department, and the executive branch absorbs some functions of a fifth department. As long as the five functions operate in a balanced manner, the organization will show the highest performance and be satisfactorily productive; otherwise, there would only be scandal, corruption, and incapability.

The Five-Star System is also the best diagnostic instrument for determining the health condition of any organization. One of my associates counseled a major U.S. bank regarding its heavy investments in a certain South American country. He was sent there to examine the situation. In one week he diagnosed the problem and came up with all the corrective suggestions. Unfortunately, the bank did not appreciate his wonderful method and sent a group of so-called experts to the same location. It took them one year to learn what the problems exactly were. By the time their reports were completed the company in South America had already collapsed. The bank lost all its investments. Later the bank admitted that the diagnostic sections of the reports submitted by my associate and the experts were exactly the same. The only differences were that my associate's report included corrective solutions and was completed within a week and the experts' report offered no solution and was completed within a year. The bank spent a great fortune acquiring a great loss, just because it lacked this knowledge.

The structures of the world's different organizations vary. Usually many managerial theories emphasize structural form; some even attribute success or failure to structural correctness or incorrectness. The result: enormous amounts of time, capital, manpower, and other resources are spent or wasted in efforts to restructure the organization to improve performance. At times these give a temporary stimulation, only to have the same problems recur immediately. In actuality the root of the problems is never touched: the imbalanced function, the heart of the problems, is often overlooked. But the moment this is diagnosed, the moment positive results are seen and problems are solved.

On the subject of structure, it is believed that the Yellow Emperor organized his government into five departments. Unfortunately there is not enough conclusive evidence establishing this as fact.

During the height of the first golden age, the Han Dynasty, the government was a model of Taoist theory. The resulting structural arrangement, shown below, has been lauded centuries after by countless scholars:

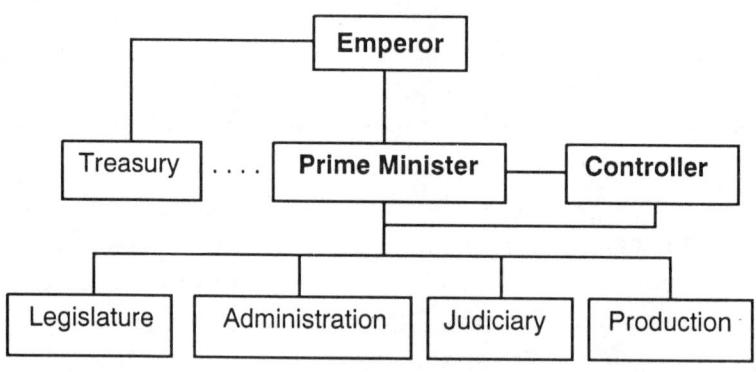

Figure 5.11

In this model, the emperor represents the state, occupies the seat of highest honor, but has no right to participate directly in state affairs. He must be a sharp judge of ability, appointing only prime ministers and controllers of exceptional merit. And he owns the state treasury (but has no right to appropriate funds). Under the prime minister are combined the powers of the legislature, administration, and judiciary. The controller is the governmental "watchdog" who brings the powers of investigation, impeachment, and indictment to bear upon the prime minister. His sole purpose is to accuse the prime minister of wrong doing, the lack of evidence notwithstanding, and report his findings to the emperor. The prime minister's salary is equivalent to one thousand *tan* of rice, the highest salary in the country. The controller's salary is equivalent to two hundred *tan* of rice. If the emperor accepts the controller's accusations, the prime minister must leave, whether or not he is guilty as charged. The prime minister cannot contest this decision, because he has ample opportunity to dissolve any suspicions of wrong doing, so he must accept the consequences of his failure. And because he occupies a post of such honor, he is above vindication by the courts; only history can vindicate him if he is innocent. His work is immediately and automatically inherited by the controller. A new controller is appointed by the emperor to watch the new prime minister.

This system is modeled after Lao Tzu's famous theory: *Yu-wei, Wu-wei, Wu-pu-wei*, again, meaning "Doing everything, doing nothing, everything can be done." The prime minister manifests *Yu-wei* because he has power to do all. The emperor manifests *Wu-wei* because he has power to do almost nothing. Together with the controller they manifest *Wu-pu-wei* because they can accomplish state affairs with the highest efficiency, thoroughness, and correctness. All of their powers are checked, balanced, and enhanced by a structure that preserves the functions and optimizes performance and productivity. (The last time this structure was used was during the zenith of the second golden age, the T'ang Dynasty. The rest of Chinese history showed a steady decline, as greedy and selfish heads of state embraced other theories and forms of government for their own benefit.) Most fascinating is the unity of the legislative, administrative, and judicial powers in this system. There are no conflicts resulting in incapability. Instead there is only capability, since the abuses of power are eliminated by the controller. In modern terms, the functions of the emperor are very much like those of the chairman of the board; those of the prime minister, the president. The last and most important point is that the five functions can be preserved perfectly in any structural form, as long as that structure does not strangle or cut off any of those functions.

CHAPTER 6

THE TAO OF PSYCHO-DYNAMICS

At about 500 B.C. the scholars of ancient China began debate on the issue of human nature. Human nature bears great significance upon management, because policy is determined by what human nature truly is. If human nature is intrinsically good, then all one needs to do is trust subordinates, respect them, reward them, support them, uncover and encourage their good nature and creativity. And they will naturally return these kindnesses with excellent and faithful service. If human nature is intrinsically evil, then subordinates must be destructive, lazy, and irresponsible and must always be watched and punished. Recently the famous Theory X and Theory Y have been bringing to light such assumptions about human nature.

Mencius was the one who first brought up the issue that human beings were intrinsically good. His management style developed accordingly from this central idea (he contributed greatly to the Scholar Style of Management). People loved accepting an optimistic concept that emphasized only the bright side.

Against such views were those of Hsin Tzu, who was the scholar who first brought up the evil side of human nature. His theory, like the theory of the sons of Adam and Eve, maintained that everybody was born evil. Many people used his strategies but were unwilling to admit they thought human beings were evil.

Countless times I have searched through the texts of Taoism, hoping to discover which point of view it is more apt to support. Actually, a point of view will never be found because Taoist scholars have never bothered to take sides in the arguments over good and evil. To them, good and evil are relative factors, and *absolute* good and *absolute* evil do not exist. If we set up management policies based on concepts that are nonexistent or irresolute at best, it is no wonder that there have been so many failures and so much frustration.

The fact is human psychology and behavior change their course in accordance with the rules of Psycho-Dynamics. The Taoist scholar Lee, Chung-Wu (1871-1937) explained these quite clearly.

He began by criticizing two situations presented by Mencius in support of his Good-Human-Nature Theory. The situations are as follows: "All the little children love their parents. When they grow up, they love their brothers," and "A baby crawls near a well. Whoever sees this must be filled with apprehension and sadness." Lee, Chung-Wu presented a case that conflicted with the first situation: "Let us test a child by putting him in his mother's arms when she is eating. When that child sees that his mother is eating something, he never hesitates to reach out and pull the plate of food towards himself. He may even pull it off the table, smashing it to pieces. Again, if his mother holds a piece of cake in her hands, he will immediately reach out to grab the cake and put it in his own mouth.

Now if his brother comes and tries to grab a piece of that cake from his mother, he will try to push his brother away. If that brother refuses to leave, he may try to hit him and cry." Can all these actions be called love or good nature?

If we know these actions to be evil in nature, how can we satisfactorily explain the examples presented by Mencius to be true? How can we ignore the true incidents of good nature?

We will forever be troubled by this paradox as long as we must establish one situation to be true over the other.

A better understanding is gained by passing on and looking at what are called "Magnetic Fields," which share the common center "I." Let us pretend we are that child for a moment. As that child we would unconsciously know: "*I* am the center of my world. Everything occupies a field that surrounds me." Therefore, according to Scholar Lee, whatever is closer to us takes precedence over whatever is relatively further away from us.

If the child places himself in the center and places his mother in the field closest to him, the child will place himself first and grab the cake from his mother. When a field is formed outside his mother's to include his brother, he will chose his mother—regarded as closer to him—over his brother and will try to push him away. When he grows older and meets his neighbor, he will place the neighbor in a field outside that of his brother. When an incident between the neighbor and his brother forces him to chose sides, he will naturally side with his brother, because his brother is closer to him. If he travels to another village and encounters his neighbor, his bond toward his neighbor will naturally be stronger than his bond toward the villagers. The number of fields grows ever larger until his country is included in the outer peripheries. Then, when he must choose between his country and a foreign country, he will choose the country that is closer to him.

THE TAO OF PSYCHO-DYNAMICS

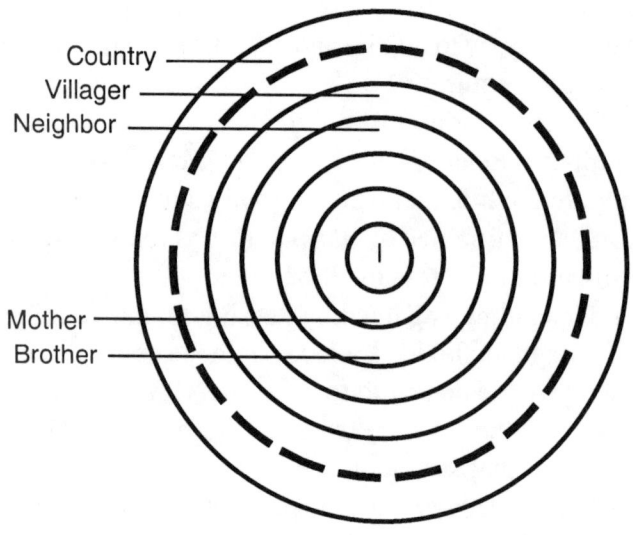

Figure 6.1

The series of Magnetic Fields can be read in both directions, from the center outwards and from the outer peripheries to the center. Nothing that a person comes across in his or her life escapes this kind of "fielding."

To further the understanding of Psycho-Dynamics, Scholar Lee presented the following series of comparisons which take us from the peripheries to the center. Suppose we are taking a walk on a beautiful spring day, and the panoramic views of many-hued rolling mountains, fertile valleys, gleaming rivers and lakes against an azure sky fill us with awe for the mighty universal forces that shape our universe. All of sudden, our eyes focus on a desolate scene of shattered rock, and we completely forget about the magnificence of the universe. A wave of feelings take hold of us, ranging from dislike of the unappealingness of the rocks to regret for whatever destruction might have occurred. But as we continue to walk, we happen upon a patch of flowering plants. The petals of the beautiful flowers are, one by one, dropping onto the shattered rocks. Immediately our attention is focused on the fallen flowers, and a wave of pity seizes us, making us forget completely about the rocks. Further away we see that upon the carpet of petals lies a wounded dog. Immediately our attention and waves of feelings are riveted on the dog, and we forget about the fallen flowers. The dog occupies a field still closer to us. But then as we walk further, we see a dog attack a human being, a stranger. Nevertheless, without a second thought, we jump to the man's aid. Of all the fields so far, the field occupied by the human being is closest to us. As we near our village, we see our friend being beaten by a stranger, and spontaneously we rush to help him. A little while later, as we sit comforting our friend in our house, we see that the roof is about to collapse on top of us. Immediately we run out, calling back to the friend to run. We are at the center of all our fields.

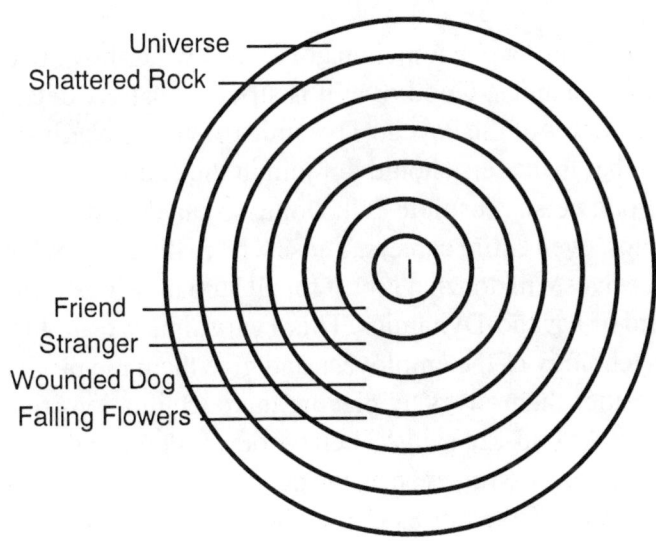

Figure 6.2

The Tao of Psycho-Dynamics

No matter what the situation is, an inflexible factor influencing the outcome is the central character "I." The specific way human beings perceive and weigh their priorities and behave in response to them is called Psycho-Dynamics. Two rules of Psycho-Dynamics are:

1) Centripetal Perception: The closer something is in relation to an individual, the greater the individual's affinity towards it will be.

2) Centrifugal Perception: The further away something is, the lesser the affinity will be.

Seen in the context of the rules of Psycho-Dynamics, the second story told by Mencius is known to be valid. We naturally feel apprehension and sympathy for the baby who crawls near a well. Our attention is riveted on the baby instead of the well because the baby is human, not matter. It belongs in a field that is closer to us than the well.

Human nature is just a phenomenon governed by the above two rules of Psycho-Dynamics. Good or evil is strictly relative, determined by the standards of the Psycho-Dynamics of various individuals. It follows that managers should not join in the endless debate over absolute good versus absolute evil. Doing so can destroy business relationships, even entire careers. Those who really know what is best for themselves will do what is best for all human beings—the highest standard of Psycho-Dynamics. This a very simple task. Just observe the psychology of the employees and give them the proper stimulation to better themselves by placing them in situations that exactly suit them. As Lao Tzu said, "Their work was done, and their undertakings were successful, even as the people all say 'We are as we are of ourselves.'" Take, for example, the case of two enemies who are caught in a small boat alone in a stormy sea. These two will put aside their differences and work together as brothers to secure their lives. Likewise, two brothers who fight for an inheritance and are bitter enemies will immediately join forces when an enemy attacks. After the enemy is vanquished the brothers will resume their infighting. What is called "helping," "unity," "good," "disagreement," "fighting," or "evil" is purely circumstantial.

In physics, qualities equivalent to these are represented by the component and resultant forces.

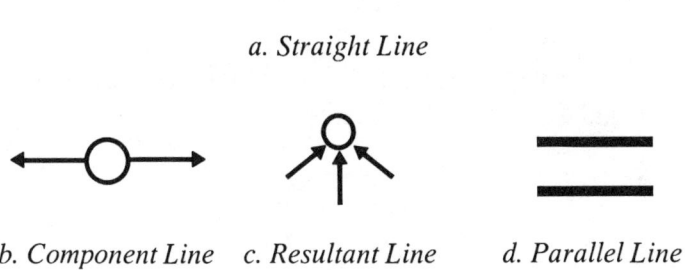

a. Straight Line

b. Component Line   c. Resultant Line   d. Parallel Line

Figure 6.3a-d Straight Line and its related interactions, as shown by the Component, Resultant, and Parallel Lines.

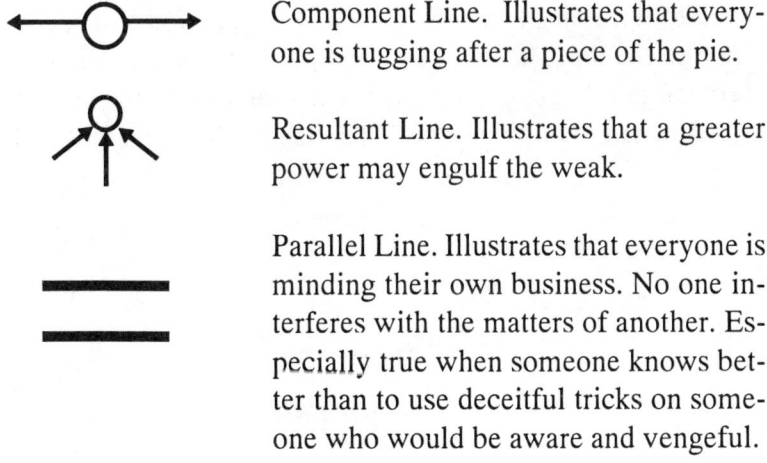

Component Line. Illustrates that everyone is tugging after a piece of the pie.

Resultant Line. Illustrates that a greater power may engulf the weak.

Parallel Line. Illustrates that everyone is minding their own business. No one interferes with the matters of another. Especially true when someone knows better than to use deceitful tricks on someone who would be aware and vengeful.

Further insight is provided as to how human interactions usually work out once human beings have determined their relationships—or fields of affinity—with respect to each other. The five major patterns are best represented by the five analytic geometrical forms:

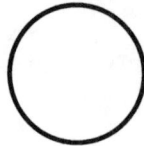

Figure 6.4 Circle

Illustrates that everything in this universe has been prearranged. Everyone and everything belongs to a field defined by a circle.

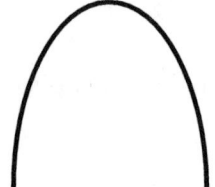

Figure 6.5 Parabola

Shows that one launches oneself with great force to begin one's climb to the top. But as one rises higher and higher, inabilities or shortcomings begin to pull one down, as one is unable to overcome their downward pulling force. Then one finally succumbs and falls.

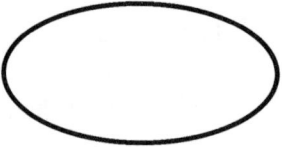

Figure 6.6 Ellipse

The Tao of Psycho-Dynamics

Illustrates how one, starting at one point but dissastisfied, seeks out other alternatives. But after an extensive search, one comes back to the point where one started. Deal making is governed by this nature.

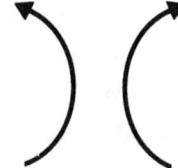

Figure 6.7 Hyperbola

Illustrates how those who take sides in a particular issue never meet at one point. They may come close to agreeing but the distance between both sides will always be there.

Finally with thorough understanding of the knowledge given, managers will be able to apply the following powerful technique masterfully.

Figure 6.8 Sun (or "Loss") Hexagram

Illustrated above is the hexagram for loss (more information may be found in *The Great Tao*), which represents a powerful technique. It can be described as follows: Contrariness involves only two parties (Yin and Yang). A third party cannot exist. Everything boils down to two parties which contend with each other until one party prevails over the other. If, for example, there really are three parties—A, B, and C—two will always team up to form a whole against one. A and B unite against C. C will lose and will gradually be reduced to zero. Then A and B will contend. To eliminate B, A must split B into opposing forces E and D. If E is eliminated, D is left. To eliminate D, A must split D apart. When all opposition is eliminated, A itself will split into two opposing forces. Contention goes on forever. In the practical world, this technique can be as powerful as a two-edged sword. Managers cannot survive without knowing it.

To be a successful manager is to be knowledgeable of these universal laws and be able to arrange the physical surroundings accordingly. God is a great manager. He set the sun, moon, planets, stars in their proper positions, so that they occupy different fields according to their gravities. In human society, if you know every individual's power of gravity and place everyone in the proper fields, then everybody will be happy and give his or her best performance and highest productiveness.

PART II

LOFTY PERFORMANCE

Chapter 7

The Tao of Leadership

In Part I of this book, we have laid the groundwork for achievement by showing how a right person, with the right attitudes, in the right place, and with the right people, would be well prepared. Now we come to the more important and critical part: doing the right thing the right way.

First of all, a leader cannot do anything right without leadership. Leadership is a matter of importance not only to the achievement of the leader, but also to the benefit, happiness, and life existence of those dependent upon it. MBA degrees are important, but not failing yourself or others in the practical world should be more important, even critical. The following story illustrates this point.

During World War II there was a general, Commander Chang, who was responsible for protecting and maintaining the Canton division of the vital Yuei-Han Railway, which transected the Hupai, Hunan, and Canton Provinces. He was also responsible for keeping all other traffic arteries in Canton open, in order to supply the defending armies at the front and keep the economy of Canton and other provinces alive.

At the time of our story, Hupai was already lost to enemy occupation, and Hunan was being bombarded by Japanese planes. Many bridges were destroyed, including the one near Hsian-Tang. This particular bridge—the one and only bridge—supported not only the defending armies' main supply route across the wide and rushing Hsian River, but also the entire Hunan economy. If it were damaged the armies at the front and the Hunan populace would face annihilation. But six hundred feet of the bridge, right above the middle of the river, was destroyed, making repairs extremely difficult.

Pressure from all sides descended upon Commander New, head of the Hunan Railway and Transportation Division, to repair the bridge. Headquarters ordered Commander New to repair the bridge in one week. But ten days passed without any sign of progress—and the armies at the front desperately needed supplies. Both Commander New and headquarters at the war capital telephoned and telegraphed Commander Chang for immediate aid.

Before dawn, Commander Chang arrived at the construction site, checked the situation, and called the two engineers, who had been bitterly disagreeing with each other from the beginning, to report on the situation and listen to their suggestions. After a quick breakfast at dawn, he went to see Commander New in his quarters, surprising him with his prompt arrival. He told New he thought he could finish the repair construction in three days. New could not stop shaking his head in disbelief, but finally said he would do everything in his power to support Commander Chang if such a miracle could possibly be performed.

Commander Chang immediately set to work. First he asked New to immediately pay the laborers the wages owed them, whether they deserved it or not. Commander New protested that if the workers got their pay, they would not report for work the next day; that these workers were not professionals but were locals hired because the enormity of the task left the professional maintenance workers short-handed; that the locals did not understand the importance of the task and made excuses whenever possible to avoid coming to work; that they grabbed the easiest jobs when they did show up for work; that they seriously diminished the working spirit of those who did work; and that the situation was made worse by the two fighting engineers who could not agree on how the bridge was to be repaired. Nevertheless, Commander Chang insisted that the workers be paid, while promising Commander New that he would assume full responsibility if anything went wrong.

After Commander New announced the distribution of pay, every one of the two hundred workers showed up, and that was when they heard Commander Chang's speech. They were told that he would be working with them from then on; that he planned to have the construction finished in three days; that they would be paid the highest wages; that if work was finished on time, there would be two days' worth of extra pay (bonus) for each worker; that anyone who neglected to show up for work or work hard would be punished severely by military law; that Commander New would be watching and checking up on them; that he would be camping with all of them on the river bank; that they would eat together and sleep together; that they would have a big banquet, prepared by Commander New; that they would start work early next morning; that everyone would rest come break-time and work come work-time; that those who disobeyed orders would be punished for disobedience and disrupting order.

At this point Commander Chang divided the workers into twenty groups (each group consisted of ten men headed by a foreman) and made each group responsible for thirty feet of repairs. He also made each engineer responsible for three hundred feet of repairs and the supervision of ten foremen and one hundred workers. The engineers were instructed to go directly to him if there were any problems, since he would always be with them.

Then he resumed his speech, saying that he was paying them to repair the bridge; that the bridge belonged to everybody, especially the local residents; that if the bridge were not repaired on time, they and their families would suffer a horrendous fate at the hands of the enemy; that the soldiers at the front would not get any supplies and lose the battle against the enemy; that the enemy would take their land and property; that the enemy would repair the bridge for his own use by chaining them and working them to death as slaves; and that their wives and children would suffer the unspeakable fates that the entire nation was witnessing. Thus ended his speech.

Afterwards, Commander Chang summoned the twenty foremen to his temporary quarters, sat down with them, and encouraged and comforted them. He ended the speech on this note: all their neighbors and enemies would laugh at them if they could not even fix a simple bridge on time.

Early next morning, everyone worked according to plan, working hard into the evening. As everybody sat on the river bank, having finished dinner and having nothing to do, the urge to work seized everybody, and they begged to work for an additional three hours before it got dark.

Before three days were up, the bridge was completely repaired. Everyone was extremely happy. The armies at the front won a big victory, the famous Chang-Sha victory of the Sino-Japanese war. Commander New was promoted to another area. Commander Chang was promoted to manage the railway divisions in both the Canton and Hunan provinces, besides getting another star pinned on his shoulder.

This commander happened to be my grandfather. On my summer break I had the fortune of following him to the construction site and witnessing all that had happened. I still remember how awed I was over how a good leader with a good plan, intelligent decisions, knowledge and control of people, and enthusiastic motivational skills could completely turn things around. Certainly the world would be a much better place if there were more leaders of this kind.

Is it true that leaders are born with leadership qualities? I believe the answer is no; otherwise, why have business schools and other related schools existed until the present day? Since leadership can be trained, the question then becomes: Where can a comprehensive knowledge of leadership be found; or does it exist at all? The answer, fortunately, is yes. It is found in the form of a book handed down by the Yellow Stone Sage 2,200 years ago. Called *Su Shu*, *"The Plain Book,"* it revealed in full the wisdom and practical knowledge of leadership. It overshadowed all other books of this nature in scope and incisiveness. It came to us under rather peculiar circumstances, according to the historical records repeated here.

After the sixth kingdom was destroyed by who was to become the first emperor of the Chin Dynasty, Chin Shih Huan, China came under one rule. But one of the nobles of the defeated Kingdom of Han, Chang, Liang, was anxious to exact revenge upon the Emperor. He spent all his wealth seeking professional assassins. When one was finally found, the assassination was planned to take place during one of the Emperor's regular inspection tours. But on that fateful day, the assassin's arrow plunged into a decoy carriage, missing the Emperor completely. His plot having failed, Chang had to flee to the distant countryside. Depressed, he spent his days taking long walks along a river bank. One day an old man walked by, stopped in front of Chang, took off one of his shoes, threw it underneath the bridge they were standing on, then turned around and ordered Chang to climb down, pick it up, and return it to him. Astonished and angry, but pitying the old man, Chang obeyed and forced himself to climb down to get the shoe and up to return it. Then the old man ordered him to put the shoe on his foot. Chang almost wanted to hit the old man but obeyed, thinking he might as well do so since he had already done so much. The old man stuck his foot out to receive the shoe and walked away, laughing loudly and without even a word of thanks. Chang was astonished. A little while later, the old man reappeared. "Good boy," he said, "you may have some hope. Listen: five days from today, meet me here in the morning."

Still astonished, Chang uttered, "Yes, sir." Five days later Chang went to their meeting place but found the old man already there waiting for him.

The old man scolded him, "A young fellow like you, coming so late.... Shame on you! Meet me here again after five days!"

Five days later, Chang went to the meeting place before the sun rose, only to find the old man waiting for him with an angry look on his face: "After five days, come again!"

This time, Chang went to the meeting place at midnight to wait for the old man. In a little while the old man came. He smiled and said, "This is the way...." Then he handed Chang a book and said, "Read this and you will lead kings and emperors."

In answering Chang's question about who he was, the old man said, "Thirteen years later you will meet me at the foot of Ku-Chen Mountain in Shang-Tung Province. I am the Yellow Stone." Saying this the old man left, and Chang never saw him again.

This book was *Su Shu*. Chang read and meditated on the book until he reached a full understanding. Later, as Marquis Chang, he became the chief counselor of Liu, Pang, who was to become the founder of the Han Dynasty, and was honored with the highest merit of the empire. All of his knowledge and wisdom came from this book. Thirteen years later, at the foot of Ku-Chen Mountain, he found a yellow stone. He brought the stone home with him, set it on a pedestal, and paid respect to the stone everyday. Later Chang gave up his title and left with Sage Red Pine, a Taoist Immortal.

Marquis Chang was a very famous figure in Chinese history next to Chiang, Shang, the Great Duke. Both of them experienced the life patterns described by Lao Tzu as Yu-wei, Wu-wei, and Wu-pu-wei. In Chang's case, Yellow Stone Sage even gave him a special lesson to train him in endurance. Endurance was what he must have in order to receive the book's message, grasp it firmly, and practice it. True strength comes not from excitability or recklessness, but from true endurance.

The Sage broke leadership down into nine divisions of knowledge, beginning with:

I. QUALITIES OF A LEADER

The Sage called leaders the life force of organizations. At all levels of the organization, there must be leaders. Anybody with authority, regardless of rank, is a leader, as long as responsibility for other lives lie in his hands. And all leaders must have the qualities of being:

A. Pure.

B. Calm.

C. Fair.

D. Strict.

E. Open-minded.

F. Sound of judgement.

G. Tolerant.

H. Blessed with abundant common sense.

I. Knowledgeable in history.

J. Knowledgeable in geography.

K. Alert.

L. Authoritative.

And they must not:

A. Reject admonition.

B. Disregard good advice or suggestion.

C. Treat right and wrong doing equally.

D. Be arbitrary.

E. Be self-abusive.

F. Trust slander.

G. Be avaricious.

H. Be obscene.

The Sage said, "The leader who possesses one of the above negative qualities will be despised; two of them, the organization will be in disorder; three of them, the organization will incur a great loss; four of them, there will be disaster."

II. LEADER'S RESPONSIBILITIES TO HIS FOLLOWERS

The Sage listed the responsibilities of the leader. He must:

A. Comfort and settle those who think they are in danger.

B. Reverse negative thinking to positive.

C. Win back the hearts of those who rebelled.

D. Reestablish the reputations of those who are victims of unjust charges.

E. Discern the underlying causes of ambiguity or expressions of ambiguity.

F. Provide opportunities to those who are talented but ignored.

G. Suppress those who are untalented and too ambitious or pushy.

H. Search out and dismiss those who work hand-in-glove.

I. Educate those who are greedy.

J. Properly satisfy those who are demanding but deserving.

K. Encourage those who are frightened.

L. Get close to those who are knowledgeable.

M. Expose those who engage in conspiracies.

N. Adjust the working conditions of workers.

O. Punish those who intend to do unlawful acts.

P. Attract useful people from all directions.

Q. Warn those who are arrogant and unruly.

R. Reward those who are loyal and faithful.

S. Forgive the refuters.

T. Help those who make progress.

III. LEADER'S IMPRESSION ON FOLLOWERS

From the followers' viewpoint, good leaders in general will be:

A. Respectable

B. Reliable

C. Knowledgeable

E. Charitable

As a result, leaders will be fully trusted by their followers and be in favorable positions to have them fulfill their every request. A leader is only a leader because he or she can win the followers' full trust and attain a position of effectiveness. And he/she is able to do so because he/she possesses the above positive qualities and is fully responsible to the followers.

IV. DECISION MAKING

A leader is in a position that demands the making of endless decisions. The Sages called decisiveness the second nature of leadership. It is second only in importance to leadership itself. To put it another way: no decision making, no leadership. Funai Ukio, a famous author of 40 books and CEO of many corporations (such as NEC), has this to say about decision making: "99 percent of an organization's fate is decided by the decisions made by only one person at the top." This directly contradicts what the Japanese would have outsiders believe to be their management style. Many people have come to believe that decisions in Japanese corporations are made by all the members of a department, that decisions can only be reached by a consensus of followers, not the leader. The truth behind decision making, since it is undoubtedly critical to the life of an organization and its mission, will be revealed in full detail in the next chapter.

Now let us return to the story of Commander Chang. After he received orders from headquarters to go to the aid of Commander New, the first hurdle he faced was deciding whether he should help Commander New. Perhaps the construction was not the real problem; perhaps Commander New was using the construction as a bargaining chip. If this was truly so, Commander Chang had to tread carefully. He had to consider what New was bargaining for and whom he was bargaining with. If he decided not to go, then he had to prepare suitable excuses for a reply to headquarters. Or if he decided to go, he must decide whether he should assume only an assisting position instead of a commanding position or vice versa. If he did go and assume a command position, he would have to determine what the risks were for making an enemy of Commander New and whether the gains were worth making an enemy. After a few phone calls, including one to Commander New himself, it was concluded that there really was a problem at the construction site. Intelligence reports that came in also supported that conclusion, eliminating reasons for suspecting that there were hand-in-glove bargainings. Thus, in only one hour, the first decision was reached: *take the order and go.*

Then came the second decision: whether or not to assume a high or low profile. Commander Chang had no idea what phase the repair construction was in, so he rushed to the construction site to see and hear for himself. Before he went to see Commander New, he had already collected all the information on the repairs, had consulted briefly with his staff, and had produced a complete plan. Actually, in his exclusive car during the eight-hour train ride to Hunan, he and his staff had already designed plans along with contingency plans that covered all the possibilities. When the actual conditions were determined, a plan could be selected immediately, and actual decisions based on preliminary decisions could be made within a short time. Thus he was able to assume a high profile when he saw Commander New a little while after dawn.

Because he was pressed for time (he needed the workers to start work immediately and put forth their best efforts, so that the repairs could be completed within three days) and his status as a stranger was a great disadvantage, he decided he must first get all of them to trust him. The method he chose was to pay all of them the salaries that were owed them (Commander New objected vehemently to this; he withheld the workers' pay because of absenteeism and work badly done or undone). Then he decided to top this attention-grabbing gesture with a charismatic oratory performance, making the most of his communicative skills and the workers' worst fears.

The final decisions concerned the division of labor, the fair distribution of responsibilities, and the working structure with a built-in competitive function. Numerous small decisions remained until the work was completed.

The entire plan and all the decisions were aimed at having everybody win. *Everybody wins* is a golden principle of the Integral Management of Tao, because it guarantees superior performance and results. How a manager makes decisions of this nature, even though as a leader he is deluged daily with decisions (each one critical to achievement or disaster) will be discussed in the next chapter.

V. THE POWER OF THE LEADER

The power of the leader is concentrated in persuasion and reward.

A. Persuasion

If you were a VIP who was invited to a feast hosted by a king, you would need little encouragement to eat, drink, dance, or take part in the festivities. Unfortunately in the real world, most situations are rarely like royal feasts. Most people are forced to work by the state, beliefs, certain doctrines or "-isms," or simply by the basic needs for milk and bread.

A leader is needed because almost everybody out there is waiting to be pushed, encouraged, or stimulated to work. Especially if the work is boring, unwanted, unwholesome, unfavorable, unsafe, or requires special effort, then workers definitely need to be convinced and persuaded. Otherwise, the necessary work will never be done.

Whoever is capable of persuading workers to finish a job of an unpleasant nature will be called a leader. Put in another way, a leader is someone who possesses the magical skills of communication and persuasion, makes people listen to him, and makes people do things they normally would refuse to do and do it well. The Sage instructs the individual who believes himself to be a leader to "convince himself to learn the skill of communication, then maybe he will be able to hold his position, which is to convince others." The importance of communicaton as a skill of a leader cannot be overemphasized; therefore, I have decided to devote a complete chapter (Chapter 9) to this subject.

Returning again to Commander Chang's case, we find verbal strategy at work. When he decided to take charge of the repair construction, he knew that without the two hundred workers' cooperation, he could never dream of accomplishing his goal. But the failure of the first attempt at construction was due to the same workers.

(From Commander New's description, we know the workers were mostly hired from the local population. They neither needed nor cared for the bridge so they had no working spirit. They came and went as they pleased, and New had no way to control it. In addition, the two engineers were at each other's throats constantly. Even though the construction was planned to be completed in seven days, ten days had already passed and the work had yet to get past the starting point. These were the real reasons why Commander New could not wait to wash his hands of the entire matter and pass the ghastly mess to anyone willing to deal with it.)

Not only was Commander Chang brave enough to take the job, but he also tried to finish the work in three short days. Though he did not have to worry about materials or other such problems, dealing with the workers was not made easier. Nevertheless, he was confident because he had a system. He realized that worker cooperation was the only factor determining his success or failure, so he decided upon the following strategy:

> 1. He requested that the workers be paid the salaries owed, expecting that this action would bring all of them to the construction site.
>
> 2. He spoke to them when they were all present. What he essentially said was:
>
>> a. They only had to come to work for three days.
>>
>> b. They would be paid the highest wages, plus a bonus of two days' wages. Put another way, they would get five days' pay for three days' work. This was hard to refuse. And

when he offered them free food, the offer was even harder to refuse. As the Sage said, "A leader cannot lead people with empty words. Nothing is more powerful than reward."

c. He promised they would be punished by military law if they did not follow orders to work.

d. He pointed out several important facts. He was paying them high wages and many benefits to work. If they refused, they would still have to do the same work, but they would do it in chains and under severe torment. If they refused his deal, the bridge would never be repaired on time. The soldiers at the front would definitely lose the battle, being denied vital supplies by their own countrymen. The enemy would come sooner than anyone could imagine, kill their families, take their property, and then chain them to repair the bridge for their enemies' use. Commander Chang confronted them with these choices: they could work for honor or shame, money or whip, happy families or certain death.

e. He made sure the foremen took his words to heart, encouraging them to keep their honor and dignity.

This magic prescription was effective immediately—whoever remained unpersuaded had to be daff. After all was accomplished, many people praised Commander Chang for performing a miracle—repairing a bridge in three days—an impossible mission. Actually, he just knew how to convince people and utilize the principle of Psycho-Dynamics. It was as simple as that.

B. Reward

"Nothing is more powerful than reward," said the Sage. "A leader has two powerful weapons in each hand: one is reward, the other is punishment. But a good leader never uses the latter."

"Beside the bait," continued the Sage, "there must always be caught fish. Under heavy reward, the brave fighter will do anything for his benefactor. If honor is offered upon material reward, the incentive is a hundred times more powerful."

It is said that punishment should only be displayed but not used. Why is this so? Not used carefully, punishment could backfire on the user. Punishment makes people hate the user to the bottom of their hearts. Furthermore, its power is short-lived, it is much more expensive to use, and its power is very limited. The worst punishment is death, and according to Lao Tzu, if people do not fear death, what else could you do? You become completely powerless as you are out of options. Therefore, the best way to use it is to display it. After all, a whip to a lion tamer is very much like what a baton is to a conductor.

Similarly, rewards must also be used carefully. Rewards are to people what carrots are to horses. After doing tricks, dolphins are always rewarded. Rewards are powerful instruments of persuasion. However, the Sage warned, "A leader who uses rewards to motivate his people must know when to do it, how to do it, where to do it, and who to do it to. Most importantly he must let them know why he is using it." The importance of his last words is evident in the following story.

Once I had the opportunity to visit a special place for elephant training. There were many apples, bananas, potatoes, and cakes stored for rewarding an elephant after it had carried out its trainer's orders well. I saw an elephant resting alone. I thought I would show him some kindness, picked up a banana, and started walking towards him to give it to him. Suddenly, the trainer jumped in front of me and yelled at me to put down the banana. I was astonished, but later the trainer apologized and explained why he tried to stop me. He said that one never gave an elephant something for nothing. Doing so would confuse it because it would not be able to figure out what the true meaning was. Besides, an elephant had an extraordinary appetite. When mealtime arrived, it would eat tons of food. If I gave him a banana, it would stimulate his appetite, and if there had not been a continuous supply of food, he would feel insulted and get angry. That would lead to a disastrous situation. I really learned a lesson. The Sage's words echoed in my mind: "A leader should never reward anybody out of whim or goodness of his heart. Overreaction will result in a negative reaction."

Reward is a powerful instrument that allows a leader to properly motivate people to accomplish special work. It is forbidden to regard it lightly as a free gift or personal favor. Goodwill without clear purpose may turn around and bite you.

C. Being with Followers

In the military style of management, working spirit is especially emphasized. Sun Tzu, author of *The Art of War*, said these famous words: "Victory to the soldier whose mental spirit is unflinching in the face of extreme anguish." His grandson Sun, Pin, one of the famous disciples of Sage Kuei-Ku, separated working spirit into five stages. He wrote in his book (unearthed in 1972 in Shang-Tung Province): "When a person wakes up in the early morning, he has a Refreshed Spirit. As morning changes to noon, he has a Strong Spirit. In the afternoon, he becomes tired and sleepy but he still has a Wandering Spirit. When evening comes, he has only a Broken Spirit. At night, all he has left is a Continuing Spirit." All working spirits pass through these five stages.

When people have just been motivated, they all have Refreshed Spirits. When they pick up the plan and start working, they reach the Strong Spirit stage. After they have worked for a while, their spirits begin to "wander." A little while longer their spirits become "broken." In the end, they can no longer continue one step more.

From Refreshed to Continuing, at every stage the working spirit must be replenished, adjusted, and encouraged. This shall be the leader's responsibility. And in order to promote working spirit, the best strategy is to be with the workers. If a football team were to play against a strong opposing team, but its coach never bothered to show up, one could imagine how this team would fare.

If Commander Chang left after he obtained a promise to work from the workers, stayed in a posh hotel in town, drank champagne, watched shows, and only came out to the construction site to work five minutes a day while seated in a sedan chair, you could imagine the kind of work and productivity that would result. But in reality Commander Chang camped, ate, and worked with the workers. From morning to night he was there with them, always within sight. His presence had a non-verbal persuasive power. The workers were even motivated to ask for extra work in the evening. And in three days the construction was finished.

The Sage said, "A leader must give his followers the impression he is with them. One of the great leaders of old was presented with a bottle of wine. He immediately ordered the wine be poured down a well, so that all his followers could drink some. He desired to show them how fairly he was treating them; a bottle of wine was not enough to share with so many, but the spirit is. To illustrate further, if followers have no water to drink, leaders shall not utter the word 'thirst.' If followers have no place to sleep, leaders shall not utter the word 'tired.' If followers have nothing to eat, leaders shall not utter the word 'hunger.' The leader is the last to drink, rest, and eat. This is the Law of Leadership. If a leader defies this law and is unable to show his followers brotherly ties and concern, he is doomed for failure."

This reminds me of a horse and rider who try to cross a deep, rushing river. The rider must not stay on the horse's back; he must climb down and swim alongside the horse. When the horse sees that his master is beside him and leading him, he feels secure and will keep swimming. The man needs his horse to keep him afloat and in position. If the man asks the horse to tackle the river alone, both will drown.

D. Budget

A limited budget is always a big concern of the leader. If he can embark on a mission with an unlimited budget, he will have a much smaller headache. Limited budgets are always big challenges for a leader. On the one hand, the leader has to motivate people to work and must reward them generously. On the other hand, money is tight. How do you cook a meal from thin air? To make matters worse, the Sage said, "The hero will be destroyed by numbers."

The leader, then, must do some creative juggling. In Commander Chang's case, a budget projected for seven days' labor was set aside for construction by headquarters. Because of the way work was organized, Commander Chang estimated construction could be completed in three days. The workers were paid five days' pay for three days' work. He spent little more than the budget for five days' work, completed the repairs, and saved the taxpayer money for almost two days' work. Everyone won in this case. Sage Chuan Tzu prescribed the following formula: when three cups of food in the morning and four cups of food in the evening are unsatisfactory, reverse the order and give four cups in the morning and three in the evening.

VI. ORGANIZATION

To ensure that a leader's plan is completely and properly carried out and that the working spirit may be constantly maintained, a favorable and convenient working system must be set up to organize all the manpower to efficiently accomplish the mission. "A good working system or structure," described the Sage, "may be a nonverbal yet constant and powerful motivator. Nothing is more important than instituting a good system before work begins."

Let us study Commander Chang's working system, beginning with the following plan drawn for organizing people and work.

Every group of ten men was responsible for thirty feet of repairs. Each group was under the supervision of a foreman. Ten foremen reported to one engineer, and each of the two engineers was responsible for three hundred feet of repairs. The two engineers reported to Commander Chang.

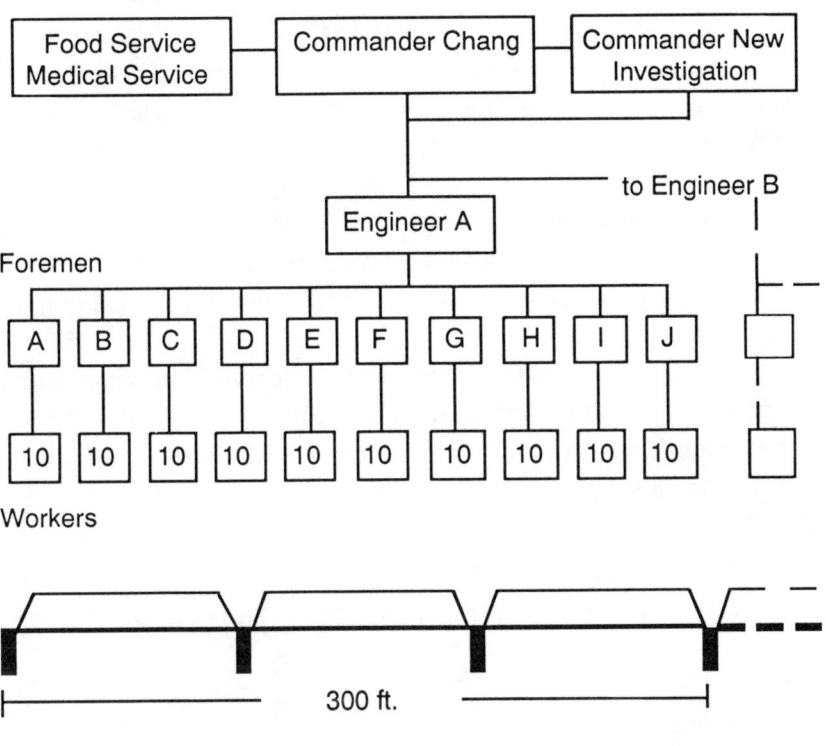

Figure 7.1

Prior to such an arrangement, two hundred workers had poor records of attendance, which Commander New could not control. Morale among those who did show up for work was low; only the easiest jobs were done. And the two engineers were arguing bitterly, because responsibility was not delegated to anyone.

When the working structure was changed, everybody was placed in their proper positions, responsibilities were clearly divided, and accountability and worker performance were easily established. Everybody, now part of a Five-Element Department or Five-

Element Function, was working at optimum efficiency.

Another interesting and important point about the system is the built-in competition motivator. For example, neither the engineers nor the working groups were willing to finish last in their class and lose face. Once the working spirit was ignited it automatically refueled and reignited itself without another word from Commander Chang. Neither was Commander New left out; he was assigned a nice and easy job to save face. If the mission was accomplished, Commander New shared in the honor. As one can see, nothing was left to chance. Everything was well-considered and well-organized, and everybody was placed in a winning position—the ideal goal of management.

Looking back at those events, one may be mildly astonished that the professionally and scientifically executed strategies of contemporary planners were actually executed according to the guidelines of the ancient scholarly teachings of Taoism.

VII. SACRIFICES OF THE LEADER

A. Loneliness

Loneliness becomes more and more pronounced as the rank of leadership reaches ever higher.

It has been explained earlier that followers want their leaders to be authoritative, or in other words, show a side that is stern and powerful.

In the home environment, the role of the leader is assumed by the father. In order to educate the children well, a father plays the stern, authoritative role. The children are scared and dare not disobey instruction. But the severity of the relationship may cause the children to retroact or come to fear the masculine figure. That is why the presence of a mother figure, if she brings a tender balance to the harshness of the father, is so important. When she constantly reminds the children that their father's actions arise out of love and concern for them, the father's efforts to instruct them will be ten times more powerful. Respect and order will be maintained, and the entire household benefits. But if the mother's character is harsher than the father's, the children will run away. And if the father's character is softer than the mother's, all the children will be completely spoiled.

In the working environment, if the superior plays the father's role, he needs someone to play the mother's role. If he plays the mother's role, someone is needed to play the father's role. But in reality, the perfect working partner does not exist, leaving the superior in a potentially dangerous situation. So he has no choice but to play both roles alone. At times he is stern, distant, and authoritative; at other times he is caring. If both roles are played well, orders are obeyed without any alienation of subordinates.

The superior must be whole unto himself; he must play both major and supportive roles alone. He must distance himself from subordinates to maintain an aura of authority and to garner respect so that his orders will be obeyed. Furthermore, he must never let his emotions for others affect his business decisions. If he does, then the entire organization, all the people dependent upon it, and his own dignity will be sacrificed. Thus a leader must have a herculean capacity for bearing loneliness.

B. Freedom

The higher the leader's rank, the more he can accomplish or obtain. But little freedoms such as going where he wishes, associating with whom he desires, saying what he wishes, and so on must be given up.

C. Security

The higher the rank of leadership, the more tenuous the feeling of security.

If people trust their leaders and rely on them, they feel secure as long as their leaders are with them. The leaders of lowest rank rely on their leaders, who in turn rely on their leader. The topmost leader has no one else to lean on but himself.

When a leader climbs up the leadership ladder, he gains more knowledge and wisdom, expands his known territory, and encounters and understands more dangers that previously lie hidden. As he gains more experience, he becomes more cautious. As he climbs higher, the view of his responsibilities grows larger, and he dares do less and less. He seems to lose his abilities as his status grows. As the Sage said, "Everyone needs to be constantly reminded that at the bottom too much freedom [daring to do anything] may obstruct one's advance, and at the top too much fear obstructs one's advance."

VIII. COUNTERACTION

There are three big obstacles that counteract good leadership, dissolving all the effectiveness and efficiency invisibly and easily.

A. Scheme of Pretense

The subordinates do not object to any of the superior's orders. They observe the rules and seem to obey, but they ostensibly take orders without ever intending to execute them. If the superior insists upon a reason for the inactivity, the subordinates will make all possible excuses and procrastinate until the mission is worn down. Once a superior is dragged into such muddled circumstances, rarely will he be able to extract himself. If such circumstances are found in an organization, that organization is incompetent. If they are found in government, that government is incompetent. Said the Sage, "Wherever this scheme is used, the leader is to blame." An incompatible leader causes incompetence, and the root of this disease is greed. "Greed leads to inferiority."

B. Scheme of Jurisdiction

The Taoist scholar Lee, Chung-Wu told this story: "Long ago, there was a certain doctor. One day a patient came to see him with an arrow buried in his arm. The doctor took a saw and sawed off the arrow stem and bandaged the arm with the arrow head still in it. The patient was furious and rebuked the doctor for the inadequate treatment. But the doctor replied nonchalantly, 'I'm only an *externist*. The arrow head falls under the jurisdiction of the internist.'"

When a subordinate obeys an order by executing a particular part of it, while purposely leaving another part (perhaps the most important part) unexecuted, he is using the Scheme of Jurisdiction.

This scheme is crueler and more vicious than the preceding scheme. Instances of its use can be found throughout history and throughout the world. It is perhaps the most popular scheme ever invented.

In some cases, people may just be too scared to "dig the arrow out"—that is, get to the bottom of the entire problem. No one dares to get to the bottom of the problem because no one dares to open a Pandora's boxful of problems. They would rather patch up the surface and improve the appearance. This is true when leaders play politics. For example, solving the government deficit is a problem no one dares tackle because no one dares to open the proverbial can of worms. The only wise thing that could be done is to cry loudly for diminishing the deficit.

Applying bandages is practiced in every household, even in the Kingdom of God. God only punishes evil people. Why does he not eliminate the Devil in the first place? The answer may be found in Chapter 2. The Sage said, "It will be excused, as long as the practitioner is without bad intention." Therefore, the pragmatists may rest their minds in peace.

C. Swindling Scheme

If, for example, a man suspects a problem with his car, he will drive it to a nearby station for inspection. The mechanic does not find anything wrong with the car, but tells its owner that it is in good shape, except for a badly worn pipe that may cause the car to break down on the freeway. The man tells the mechanic to change the pipe. Appreciative of the mechanic's kindness, he praises the mechanic in front of his employer. In reality there is nothing wrong with the pipe, but if the mechanic tells the man the truth, the man may drive his car to another station thinking the mechanic is incompetent. In other cases, the problem may be purposely enlarged. Such schemes are second only to the Scheme of Jurisdiction in popularity. It is used to keep positions, get promotions, heighten wages, etc. As a form of political blackmail, it is especially used in international diplomatic affairs.

All the schemes described are shadows that are inseparable from the substance of any normal leadership. A good leader senses a scheme from the beginning, before anyone has a chance to use it on him. His sharpness already penetrates through the set up and immobilizes it. A leader with such perception relies on the skill of intercommunication, which will be discussed in detail in Chapter 9.

IX. GRADES OF LEADERSHIP

According to Lao Tzu there are four categories of leadership. First and highest are those leaderships that people do not know exist. Second follows those that people love and praise. Third are those that people fear. Last are those that people hate and subvert. Let us look more closely at these leaderships, beginning with the worst.

A. Leadership of Hate

The leadership is heading in the wrong direction, against the rules of true leadership. The followers are getting no benefits from the leader, who is selfish and foolish. In the end, his retribution will be hatred, humiliation, and retaliation.

B. Leadership of Fear

The leader has adopted the theory that human beings are born evil and must be driven by punishment. This leader strikes his people with terror, so that the only thought in their minds is to flee. But history has proven that a tyrannical system never lasts long.

C. Leadership of Happiness

The leader practices the principles of Taoism. People are benefiting and are happy, so they love and praise their leader.

D. Leadership of Invisibility

After a long period of rule by a Leadership of Happiness, the people completely forget that their leader even exists. This lapse of memory is the highest accolade a leadership can hope to attain. Why? Leaders are most susceptible to corruption by power, and the subjects are the first to taste the blade of corruption. The subjects who are never made to suffer, who are never troubled in the least by their leader, forget their leader exists. They are fortunate indeed, for their leader has attained the highest level of management, a form of management that is neither too light nor too heavy but is exactly right.

Emperor Yao (2333-2234 B.C.), after ruling for fifty years, suddenly wanted to know what his subjects thought of him. He first asked his servants, who answered they did not know. He then asked his ministers, who also did not know.

He decided to find out for himself, so he disguised himself and ventured out among his subjects. In the cities and villages he heard the children sing: "We live so happily, but know not whence our happiness comes. We do not have to know, just let us flow with it as long as we may." The old men also sang: "When the sun rises, we work. When it sets, we rest. We dig wells to drink, harvest to eat. We need not know if there is a king." Emperor Yao was a Sage. Throughout the millenniums that followed, he was considered to be the epitome of great leaders.

I remember that Takuya Hatoyama of Janome Industry in Japan once said, "All of the Japanese corporations should adopt this style of management as our highest goal, so that the feelings of pain and heaviness will be lifted from our employees and that our working strategy becomes just right, neither too light nor too heavy. This has been my life-long goal."

Chapter 8

The Tao of Complete Resolution

According to the Yellow Emperor, the human mental body has three functions: feeling, thinking, and decision making. The three functions originate from five organs: the heart, liver, lungs, spleen, and kidneys. The brain only records and directs the functions. (Why this is so is explained in *The Complete System of Self-Healing: Internal Exercises*.) The five organs' direct connection (via the Central Nervous System) to the brain and their influence upon the brain serve as the basis for the formulation of the theory of the Five-Element Personalities. Infinite implications arise from such a connection. For example, it is known that dysfunctions of a particular organ are directly correlated with particular mental dysfunctions. If the lungs are diseased, emotional feelings become intensified to an extreme degree. If the heart is diseased, intuitive thoughts or psychic capabilities are diminished. If the liver is diseased, the thinking process will be confused. If the spleen-pancreas is diseased, ponderings become excessive. If the kidney is diseased, decision making is impaired. Of the five organs that govern the mental processes, three govern the thought processes (the heart governs intuitive thought; liver, rational thought; spleen, deep thought) and only two govern the emotional and decision-making processes.

One can see, by the very nature of the above arrangements, we should be using three times more energy for thought than for the decision making that is to follow. Even so, decision making is terribly important: it is to a leader what wings are to a bird. Actually everybody in the world, from the household to the white house, from the moment the eyes open in the morning, has to make decisions. More important decisions, in general, are made by leaders because of the greater numbers of lives affected.

There are two types of decisions: right and wrong—or, in other words, good or bad. The right decisions benefit and are therefore good; the wrong decisions destroy and are therefore bad. The formula for making the right decision is this: the greater the consideration given to a decision, the better the decision will be. A decision made without thinking is absolutely absurd. No matter who you are or what kind of decision you are making, this principle holds true.

I. CLASSES OF DECISIONS

Generally people make decisions according to the following guidelines:

A. According to Law

In a civilized society, human behavior is regulated mostly by laws. In certain situations decisions have to be made in accordance with those laws—no questions asked. For example, when you drive toward an intersection and the traffic signal suddenly turns red, your only choice is to stop, whether you agree or not. If you choose to contest this law, then you will be punished. Regulations by law extend to most public affairs, from those of private citizens to top government officials. No second thoughts are necessary.

B. According to Custom

Some situations allow more flexibility. Since laws do not clearly regulate such situations, decisions are made in accordance with traditions or precedents. For example, many department-store sales are timed to holidays like Washington's Birthday. You may go shopping; or if you decide against it, you may go to the zoo instead. If you choose either of these activities, or base most of your decisions on successful precedents, you will not be wrong in most cases.

C. According to Intuition

Many people have the gift of making straight decisions without giving them a second thought. Konosuke Matsushita was known as a successful man who made decisions strictly according to "intuition." Because he did not have a chance to receive much formal education—he loved telling people he was uneducated—his good decisions were regarded as nothing short of miracles. But after reading his biography, I found that he was in fact a deep thinker, an autodidact. He was actually much more educated than those who received extensive formal educations. In many books intuitive decision making is lauded. Even so, Taoist scholars have never stated that such a method should ever be applied to important matters.

D. According to Inference

A person may make decisions based on logical deductions, creative assumptions about a certain precedent, or simply an association of ideas. If, for example, a preventive health convention is coming to town, it is likely that certain people will decide to set up booths next to the meeting places to market vitamins. The success rate resulting from this kind of decision making varies, as it is circumstantial and entails much risk.

E. According to Rational Confirmation

This kind of decision making involves a multi-layered procedure involving the collection of information, listing of possible suspicions and suppositions, and analysis. These then lead to a complete confirmation, without which a decision cannot be made. Despite the difficulty involved, a decision made by such means will yield positive results, as the rate of success is always high. (Most business decisions should belong in this category.) And it is the only kind of decision making recommended highly by Taoist scholars. An example of such decisions, Commander Chang's decision, is given in the previous chapter. In this chapter, the procedures of such decision making will be discussed in detail, namely, the collection of necessary information, raising of suspicions, making of suppositions, analysis of a field of choices to ensure suitability of final decisions, and making of a final decision. The entire procedure is the basis for a complete resolution.

II. INFORMATION

"Those who need to make resolutions," said Sage Kuei Ku, "must first weigh all possible privileges and disadvantages, so they have need for all the information they can obtain." Information is defined as certain knowledge, data, documents, news material or resources, references that are definitely needed for decision making.

A. Types of Information

From the wide field of available information the Sage isolated ten basic items that should constantly arrest a decision-maker's attention. They are:

1. Finances and assets.

2. Labor and its resources.

3. Geographic condition.

4. Law, moral codes, documents, research reports.

5. Feelings between employer and employees.

6. Brain power (of competition, of staff, etc).

7. Timing.

8. Connections and contacts.

9. Sensitive zones and topics.

10. Technique.

Without the support of the above information sources, a decision may never be reached. In the case of one corporation, this was especially true. It was having some kind of labor trouble, and someone suggested hiring part-time workers as a solution. But unfamiliarity with the concept caused many meetings to be held, which resulted only in evenly divided opinions, even though the discussions went on for weeks. Meanwhile the labor problems grew so serious that outside help had to be sought.

One of my associates suggested that management send one of the secretaries to the local library to collect all the necessary information it will ever need, because the information was already there. He even told them the section where the information may be found. The secretary brought back all the research reports, statistics, including Labor Department reports on hiring part-time workers.

All the data projected a favorable impression, and the next day the decision was made to begin implementation. Two years later, corporate executives still said that decision was the most successful one they ever made. Absenteeism was reduced, workmanship was increased, and an incredible amount of money was saved. In retrospect, undoubtedly we must give some credit to information items B and D.

B. Sources of Information

For the obtainment of information, Sun Tzu named five different sources:

1. Ordinary sources. Information can be obtained from anyone, anyplace. It could be special knowledge,

common sense, a fable, a story. It is provided whenever or wherever convenient, by whomever or whatever is present.

2. Special agents. Trained to hide in specific organizations, groups, etc., their purpose is to obtain a constant stream of specific information over a long period of time.

3. Paid informants. There may be people, already in a specific organization, group, etc. and occupying an important position, who are willing to supply specific information for a price.

4. Temporary agents. An agent can be sent to a specific person or place to get required information quickly and return immediately.

5. Misinformed agents. Through deliberately ignoring agents sent by opponents and purposely supplying them with information specially designed to help one's own plans, much more than just information may be obtained. This ranks highest among the arts of intelligence.

In a famous maxim, Sun Tzu emphasized information as an element of premiere importance in the Military Style of Management: "Knowing your own and your opponent's situation guarantees victory in every battle." In political or military conflicts, the ways of collecting information are extremely critical: a better part of the battles are in a sense intelligence battles, and life or death is decided by how correctly and quickly information is collected. Of course, corporate methods of gathering information are a little less intense, but the need for information is no less great.

The Tao of Complete Resolution

For example, Konosuke Matsushita gathered information in a very simple and inexpensive way: he never hesitated to make conversation with anyone, no matter who they were or what their rank. He said that most of the good ideas he had were inspired by casual conversations with people. These methods were used concurrently by the famous president of United Airlines, Ed Carlson, who utilized a people- and information-oriented management style. In both cases, information from ordinary sources alone provided sufficient results.

(I cannot help thinking how the events at Waterloo may have changed if Napoleon Bonaparte had known a few simple facts. He wrote in his memoirs that he had no idea what the movements of his opponents were or what the movements of his own generals were during the Waterloo campaign. Alas, a hero's tears, after all, were lost in contemplation of those to come.)

Some, to be thorough, may be concerned that too much information can cause confusion, that too much information is like no information. Such a complaint is reminiscent of the saying: "Too many books equal no book." But you can find out easily for yourself how this argument lacks logic, because as long as you keep your goals in mind, you will use only the information that is useful, no matter how much information is collected. (Information is usually divided into many different categories. Usually the category of information bearing the most value attracts the most attention.) Normally people always worry about not being able to get enough information. Why, then, should anyone worry about getting "too much" information?

The assemblage of information is only a means to a higher purpose. "Leaders should never abandon any chance to imbibe information except for certain priorities," said the Sage. The priority of priorities shall be correct usage of information—the deep thought that goes into all the possibilities. Nobody can manage anything well in the world without the ability to ponder, to think deep and far ahead.

III. THINKING PROCESS

The thinking process is comprised of three functions: suspicion, supposition, and analysis.

A. Suspicion

The Sage said, "A slight error in the beginning results in irreversible misery in the end." Therefore, a good leader must be like a detective—he must be suspicious. Not even an insect should escape his sight, according to the Sage. This way the ponderer will not neglect to list all possible circumstances that may be of disadvantage or harm to the organization or mission. These suspicions can be created by information, or information can justify or remove suspicion. If any suspicion proves to be true, the necessary actions can be taken to prevent undesirable effects.

B. Supposition

After noting all unfavorable possibilities, leaders shall next determine all angles, directions, etc. of advantage. This is the work of supposition. Everyone under heaven loves benefit and profit, but that which is beneficial and profitable darts past us like a swift arrow—only the sharpest can catch it. So we are advised by the Sage to let our bait penetrate into deep waters in order to catch good fish. It is those who think deep and far ahead, not those who are asleep, who have more chances of intercepting what they desire. Hence, feats may be accomplished and battles won while others are still in a daze. Good leaders control supposition, which arise from and are confirmed by information.

C. Analysis

Both suspicion and supposition must not be based on delusions resulting from twisted imaginings, mental disorders, and so on. Instead they must arise from and be subject to deliberate analysis. At the beginning of the Han Dynasty, a method evolved from the Five-Element Theory that enriched Taoist thinking (analytic) power tremendously. It was mentioned in Chapter 6. But now the thinking process will be discussed in depth.

Suppose a subject chosen and positioned in a center is "Me," or "I."

1. Surrounding "Me" will be five types of interactional relationships, best presented thus:

   a. Question: who gives life to "Me"?
   Answer: "Parents"

   b. Q: to whom do "I" give life?
   A: "Children"

   c. Q: who controls "Me"?
   A: "Superior"

   d. Q: whom do "I" control?
   A: "Subordinate"

   e. Q: who is equal to "Me"?
   A: "Brother"

These relations are the most direct in connection to "Me" in daily living. How exactly can the five relations affect "Me"?

2. Five functions summarize the interactions between the five relations and "Me":

    a. Generates "Me." "Parents" generate "Me." For example, they nourish, clothe, please, help, teach, love, support . . . "Me."

    b. "I" create. "I" bear "Children." "I" raise them, nurture them, educate them, support them, and so on.

    c. Dominates "Me." The "Superior" is someone above "Me" whom "I" must obey, even if "I" am unwilling. As long as "I" am under his or her or its jurisdiction, "I" am dominated without choice. No matter who "I" am there will always be someone overpowering "Me."

    d. "I" control. "I" control anyone belonging under "my" jurisdiction. "I" have power over "Subordinates."

    e. Stimulates "Me." "Brothers" are "my" equals. Sometimes they compete with, help, fight . . . "Me."

For practical purposes, the meanings of the five relations are not limited to the meanings of the words themselves. For example, whatever possesses a generating function is considered to be a "Parent." Therefore, if you run your own business and the business is your livelihood (providing you with food, rent, clothing, etc.), the business has a generating

Table 8.1

Five-Star Relations	Broad Meanings in Application
"Parents"	Grand Parents. Elder relatives. Teacher. Senior. Globe. Country. City. Land. House. Car. Ship. Plane. Rain. Culture. Clothes. Business. Investments. Documents. Writings. Examination. . . .
"Children"	Grand Children. Younger Generation. Student. Reputation. Mood. Happiness. Language. Medicine. Religion. Entertainment. Creation. Invention. Productivity. Excreta. . . .
"Superior"	Government. Official. Police. Law. Doctrine. School. Organization. Mission. Career. Ailments. Bad parents. Enemy. Demon. Trouble. Disaster. Danger. Punishment. . . .
"Subordinate"	Spouse. Manpower. Servant. Viewpoint. Machinery. Equipment. Material. Price. Quality. Belongings. Property. Furniture. Money. Jewelry. Food. . . .
"Brother"	People. Body. Friend. Helper. Competitor. Co–worker. Potential enemy. Organs. Health aids. Toys. . . .

function and is considered to be a "Parent." Broader meanings of the five relations are given in Table 8.1.

Even the word "Me" or "I" can have broader applications. It can apply to the self, a situation, a group situation, an organization, a society, the world—whatever can be placed as the subject in the center. All the other relations are based on the subject in the center.

Whenever a situation needs analysis, the first step is to determine who or what occupies the "I" or central position. The second step is to locate all the Five-Star Relations, always keeping in mind the laws of the Five-Element Theory. (The relations are like the Five Elements in their generating and degenerating capacities.) This is done by first finding what generates, or is generated by, the central subject; then by determining the vector of Yin forces or influences—that is, finding what dominates or controls the central subject, and what is dominated or

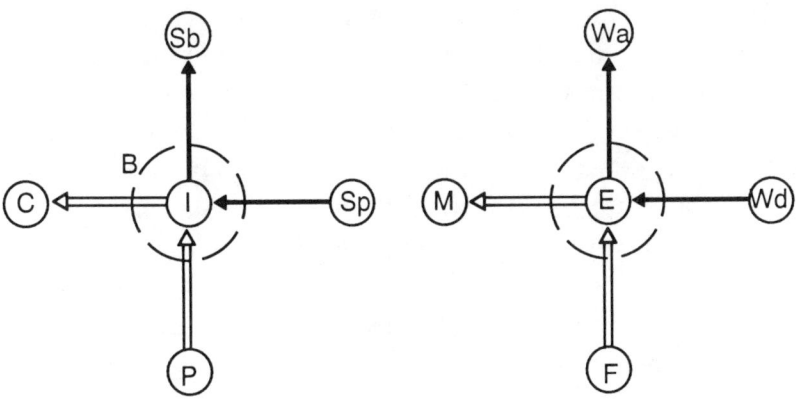

a. Five-Star Relations   b. Corresponding Elements

Figure 8.1a-b

controlled *by* the central subject. The vector of Yang forces can also be read as a relay of beneficial or advantageous influences. And the vector of Yin forces can also be read as a relay of damaging, unfavorable, or absorbing influences.

The "Brother" relation is indicated by the circle, occupying the same position as "Me" or "I," the central subject.

Through a simple charting of relevant facts, the previously obscure advantages and disadvantages are now spotlighted. New or previously raised suspicions or suppositions also show up clearly.

The third step is to weigh the strength of the Yin and Yang forces. We want to determine the strength of the "Parent" or generating force, because if it is very strong relative to "Me," it may hurt instead of help "Me." And if it is too weak, it cannot be of help either—it may be a hindrance. However, if "I" am very strong, the presence of a helpful force is inconsequential to "Me." But if "I" am weak, any bit of help is a lifesaver. For this force to be beneficial, both parties should be of equal strength or weakness. Next we determine the strength of the controlling, or "Superior," force upon "Me." If that force is too strong relative to "Me," it can completely destroy "Me." But if it is too weak, "I" will be uncontrollable and greatly trouble the "Superior." As much could be said of the other Yin and Yang vectors.

The fourth step is to check upon the relations of all involved parties as a whole, namely, the generating and controlling relations.

Let us begin by looking at a simple case of "Parent" and central subject, the case of a troubled

The Tao of Complete Resolution

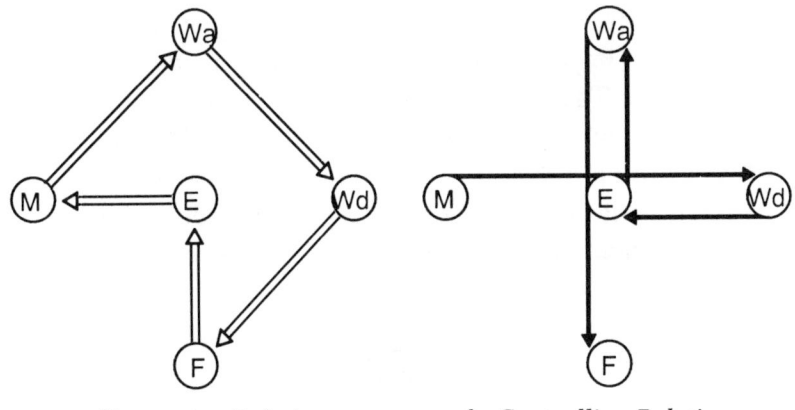

a. Generating Relation   b. Controlling Relation

Figure 8.2

teenager and his formidable parents. The parents, having gained eminent social standing and wide recognition for their substantial achievements, are much too strong in comparison to their son. Their influence upon him is one of enormous pressure to succeed. He may grow up thinking he will never measure up to them, and his self-esteem may diminish. The less self-esteem he has, the more likely he will lash out in defiant ways. He may get involved with a cult, become a drug addict, a criminal, and so on. These are the suspicions. If, however, the parents limited their social lives, etc. (to limit their own strength) or involved their son in their work (to augment their son's strength), the resulting balance would bring harmony and benefit into the relationship. These are the suppositions.

Now we will look at a more complex case. Suppose a large country (No. 1) invades a small country (No. 2) and tries to gain control over it. But the small country offers every possible advantage to another large country (No. 3) to bring it into the conflict. The latter takes every advantage from the small country and causes all possible hardships for the invading country. Meanwhile, due to the unjustness of the invasion, new concepts of morality arise throughout the world to assist the invaded country.

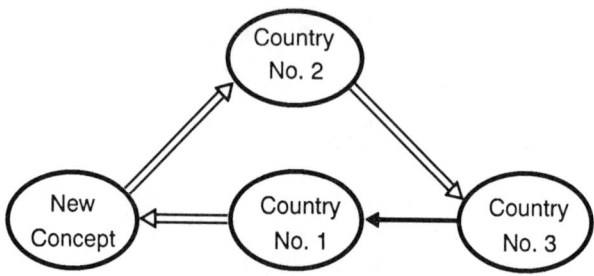

Figure 8.3 Conquest Relations

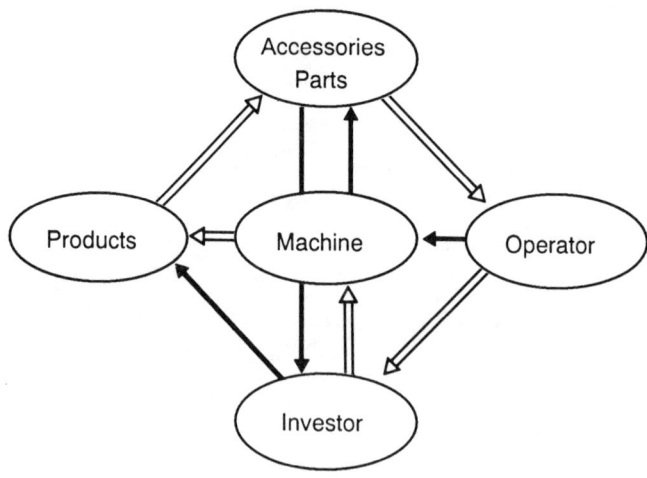

Figure 8.4 Production Relations

Last, we will examine a most complex case. Suppose the central subject is a machine. The investors buy and maintain it because they want it to produce the products they sell. The operator controls and runs it. The more the operator controls and runs it, the more products there are to sell. The more earnings there are, the more pleased the investors are. But then the machine begins to wear down, necessitating new parts and attachments. The more repairs the machine needs, the more important the operator becomes. But the expenses hurt the investors. See Figure 8.4.

This situation involves almost every function and relation, including the generating and controlling relations.

As anyone can see, any situation in the world can be easily analyzed.

3. A relation that has been left out is the "Brother." It must be discussed separately because it involves not only the concepts explained earlier, but also the Magnetic Field Theory explained in Chapter 6.

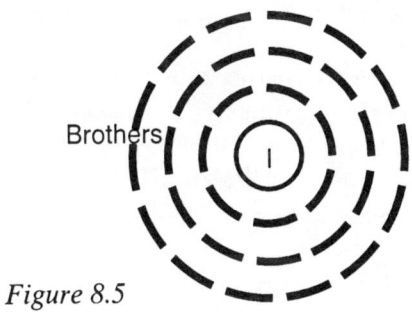

Figure 8.5

Since both "my Brothers" and "I" belong to the same element (in the Five-Element Theory), both share many similar causes. Unfortunately the results are not always the same because the Magnetic Fields occupied by each (practical positions) are different. Yellow Stone Sage listed the causes and effects of fifteen samenesses:

a. People who work for the same goal will help each other.

b. People who have the same love will be concerned for each other.

c. People who participate in the same evil doings will cover for each other.

d. People who are of the same beauty will be jealous of each other.

e. People who are of the same intelligence will scheme upon each other.

f. People who are of the same rank will inflict harm upon each other.

g. People who look for the same profit will be filled with perpetual dread of each other.

h. People who use the same kind of language can better communicate with each other.

i. People who have the same feelings will feel close to each other.

j. People who suffer the same kind of fright will depend on each other.

k. People who have the same kind of thoughts will be intimate with each other.

l. People who are attacked by the same enemy will fight the enemy together.

m. People who have the same habits will be attracted to each other.

n. People who are from the same technical field will steal from each other.

o. People who have the same talents will compete with each other.

And the list could go on.

These fundamental perceptions are the perfect tools allowing an analyzer to immediately foresee the possible results in any situation.

The Five-Star System provides us with a perfect thinking procedure for analyzing any situation. Because of it a leader will automatically think not only from his own position, but also from all other relevant positions, including those of opponents. Then he can be sure of making a decision that is perfectly right. And he can rest assured knowing he will never be victimized by his own ignorance again like the thousands of talented figures in history. It used to be that God was blamed for such failures. But why should God be blamed for their being victimized by their own blindness?

IV. COMPOSITION

The entire thinking process is very much like cooking. First all the necessary materials (or information) are gathered together and then prepared and cooked (thought out). But after cooking, the results must be arranged decoratively and served for all to enjoy. In other words, the results of the thinking process must be arranged in a composition.

It is suggested in *Kuei Ku Tzu* that when the thinking process is finished, the results should be incorporated into three compositions. Each composition is to explain each of three decisions to be chosen finally by the decision maker. Whoever the decision maker may be, whether he is the author of the composition or not, he will find all three of the decisions to be helpful. One of the decisions should be the formal decision; the other two should be the alternatives, to be relied upon in case the formal decision becomes too difficult to carry out. Each decision must, therefore, be written out fully. A composition will contain at least four paragraphs:

A. The first paragraph contains the theme (decision) and its exposition.

B. The second contains the major theory that supports the theme and the reasons—especially evidence—for that support.

C. The third contains opposing or different points of view, and the reasons and evidence explaining why the decision may or may not be acceptable.

D. The fourth is the conclusion and explains why the chosen solution should be the only solution.

This formula for composing one's thoughts is derived from Taoistic Quaternary Logic, which will be explained in the next chapter. In order for anything to be stable there must be four supporting legs, instead of three or less. Therefore, the Sage suggested that a composition be four-sectioned, to assure completeness.

Furthermore, when someone commits his thoughts to paper, he must logically review his concepts, reasons, rationales, and proofs before stringing the words together, something rarely done during conversation or simple thinking.

The formula for composition incorporates both logical induction and deduction, in addition to eliciting dialectical demonstrations. Thus, every point of view will be eventually accounted for. Until this point is reached, the "food" that is "cooked" is not ready to be "eaten."

V. FINAL DECISION

A. Three Reasons for the Occurrence of Wrong Decisions

The results of a decision can be either right or wrong. Nobody can know beforehand what the results will be; the only way to determine whether a decision is right or wrong is to wait it out after it has been carried out. Uncommonly known, the success rate of a decision can be heightened to 90 percent, if it is made in accordance with the principles described earlier. But what about the 10 percent chance of making a wrong decision? After going through so much hardship to reach a logical decision, how could things still go wrong? These are the reasons:

1. The decision is basically made against the Universal Law (for details, please refer to *The Great Tao*, Chapter 8).

2. An unforeseen accident happens after the decision is carried out. In Commander Chang's case, for

example, everything went according to plan. But if a wall of water was released suddenly from the mountains in the middle of construction, sweeping away the workers and flooding the construction site, the mission would have failed completely. Even so, the Taoist scholar will not allow people to excuse themselves for a mistake such as this, because every decision is backed up by two contingency decisions, which should include all other possible situations. When one is doing repair work on a bridge, the possibility of a flood must be taken into account.

3. The decision-maker's health is completely out of balance. At the beginning of this chapter, the functions of the brain and organs were explained. An unhealthy person will make unhealthy decisions.

God granted human beings the abilities to feel emotionally, think, and make decisions. Human beings should apply these gifts fully in order to improve themselves. Because mistakes too can be part of the learning process, they should be accepted. I wish there is a spirit or force out there waiting to be called upon to supply us with all sorts of knowledge and winning advice, but, clever readers, you should know the answer.

B. Styles of Decision Making

There are basically three known styles of decision making:

1. DECISION MAKING BY A GROUP

Voting or consensus-achieving negotiation is used by organizational members to arrive at a final decision. Demonstrations of the use of this style by some Japanese corporations were recorded by foreign cameras. Many scholars, seeing that Japanese workmanship and products were exceeding people's expectations quickly, attributed most of the improvements to this style of decision making. Actually this style has two major problems, which are explained as follows:

a. It is most effective for gaining employee feedback on plans for a corporate picnic or other special events. The thought that a corporation, in order to stay competitive in the market, would delay introducing a new product, so that *everyone* could reach a full understanding of the product and then vote or negotiate back and forth until *everyone* is absolutely convinced it will succeed, is rather ridiculous. What about corporate spies? From my observations, this style is found to be used especially by middle-level managers in over-sized corporations for destructive purposes. When a manager fears the consequences of a wrong decision, he will purposely drag all his subordinates into the decision-making process to dilute the blame.

b. If no one can be held accountable for anything, incompetence and inefficiency are the inevitable results. Actually in Japan, no theory exists recommending that such an evasive, *"Tai-Chi Chuan"* style be tolerated. But in reality if a superior chooses to play this game, a subordinate has no choice but to play with him. Such maneuverings cannot possibly be the secret behind Japanese industrial strength, in my opinion. If anything, this style of decision making is a curse.

Then what are the real reasons for the boom in Japanese productivity? After its defeat in World War II, Japan became a subjugated nation for the first time in history. The people thought they suffered a great humiliation, and a pervasive inferiority complex fueled their desire to rejuvenate their nation through dedicated work and personal sacrifice. I personally contacted many great leaders of Japanese industry, listened to their comments, and read their writings. Everywhere I found impassioned statements of indignation. The only priority in their lives is to retrieve their personal and national dignity. Simply put, it is working spirit, directed correctly, that makes Japanese products superior.

Forty years later, the sense of urgency has diminished, since the latter generations have been brought up in relative comfort. There is a great fear that complacency may diminish the competitive spirit; consequently, tremendous efforts have been directed at tightening the educational system. The pressures that drive Japanese youth are tremendous. I hope Japanese quality may remain constant for a long time.

2. DECISION MAKING BY A LEADER

Leaders exist to lead people. To lead is, above all else, to make decisions. If leaders cannot make decisions, they are not leaders. In Japan, and even throughout the world, Matsushita's decisiveness is known to be extraordinary. On the continent, Taoism has been placing great emphasis on good leaders making good decisions. Because even the best leaders make wrong decisions, the Sages have discouraged leaders from placing too much trust in their own abilities and encouraged them to arm themselves with counsel from others. The Sages condemned those who never bother to take counsel with others as a cruel autocrat. This does not mean, however, that a leader should let everyone vote on a decision; it means that a leader should do all his homework and still take counsel with others to reconfirm his rightness. Once President Abraham Lincoln asked his cabinet members to express their opinions on a particular matter. All had opposing points of view, but the President went ahead with his plans anyway. That is called leadership.

Due to the importance of leadership, the entirety of the following chapter will be devoted to the subject also.

3. DECISION MAKING BY A BRAIN TRUST

History has shown that the brain trust has been a consistent reservoir of decisions of great effectiveness and excellence. The Great Duke Chiang, Shang, whose story was told at the very beginning, was a one-man brain trust. So was Marquis Chang, Liang, whose story was told in Chapter 7. The third and most famous paragon of the one-man brain trust system was Marquis Chu-Ko, Liang, who served Emperor Liu, Pei during the Three Kingdom Period

(187-265 A.D.). Chu-Ko, Liang was a Taoist scholar with a learned reputation. To obtain Chu-Ko's consent to counsel him, Prefect Liu visited the scholar's home three times. Twice Chu-Ko avoided receiving Liu until he was deeply moved by the sincerity of Liu's third visit. So, as the Prefect's Chief Counsel, Chu-Ko helped him build an empire from nothing and made him Emperor. Chu-Ko's story became another famous testimonial for the importance of counsel.

Behind every great emperor in Chinese history stands a Taoist scholar, working behind the scenes. Only thus were achievements of the highest excellence attained, because only Taoist scholars had comprehensive knowledge of and training in management. Because their objectives were never focused on the throne, they never plotted to subvert any seat of highest honor. Their influence was one of peace and prosperity.

C. Decision Making Results

No matter what style you choose to use to make your decision, the foreseeable results can be categorized as the following:

1. Everybody wins.

2. I win and nobody loses.

3. I win and others lose.

4. Everybody loses.

THE TAO OF COMPLETE RESOLUTION

D. Optimizing Results

In order to secure better results for your decisions, Yellow Stone Sage said the following should be observed:

1. One must not be selfish and greedy.

2. One must not replace one decision with another.

3. One must not deliver less than promised.

4. One must not reject those whom one has invited.

5. One must watch for honest mistakes of this nature: different personalities hold different views, therefore make biased decisions. (Refer to Chapter 5.)

6. As the decision maker, one must do Internal Exercises to balance one's internal organs and improve the function of the brain. (If, for example, the piano is not tuned, the music that is produced will be completely dissonant. Internal Exercises are the best ways to self-tune the body. They are not limited by space or time, are easy to do, and are completely safe and effective. Doing the exercises, after a period of time, can elevate the functions of the body until it reaches the highest level of performance. Then, as Lao Tzu described, you need not set one foot out the door and you will know all that is under the heavens, and you need not look out the window to know the Tao of Heaven.) (Refer to the Appendix, Chapter 3, and *The Complete System of Self-Healing: Internal Exercises*, which was named in the April 27, 1987 issue of *Fortune* magazine as one of the "ten books bosses read.")

The Tao of Complete Resolution

About leadership Lao Tzu said, "Governing a great state is like cooking small fish. . . . It is the TAO (WAY) of HEAVEN not to strive, and yet it skillfully overcomes; not to verbally speak, and it is skillful in (obtaining) the right response; does not summon, and yet people come to it of themselves. Its demonstrations are quiet, and yet its plans are skillful and effective. The meshes of the net of heaven are large and far apart, yet it allows nothing to escape."

CHAPTER 9

THE TAO OF INTERCOMMUNICATION

I. MESSAGES

Human beings possess physical bodies. This simple fact alone is the cause of all the endless trials and tribulations in human history. Lao Tzu said, "What makes me liable to great calamity is my having this body (which I call "Myself"); if I had not this body, what great calamity could befall me?" But most unfortunately who on the face of this earth is not without a body? Everyone then must cater to the four basic physical instincts: entertainment, contention, consumption, and reproduction.

These instincts can be narrowed down to two guiding principles: 1) anything that is good for me I want; and 2) anything that is bad for me I do not want. The former is a need *to get*—Yang. The latter is a need *to avoid*—Yin. Frankly, all the things that human beings have ever done could be placed into these two categories, though the truth may not be obvious at first glance.

In order to ensure that their needs will be fully honored by others, human beings will camouflage their "need messages" various ways. Poets can compose hundreds of poems in praise of flowers (it seems to have hundreds of meanings for them), but plants cannot express their flowers in such eloquent terms. For plants flowers are direct displays of only one thing: that which forces cats to scream in late spring. Because human beings have been equipped with much more complex functions, even simple needs like those of plants and cats will be expressed much more complexly and artistically.

Because human beings also possess mental and spiritual bodies in addition to physical bodies, and because these three folds of the body are melded together, the "need messages" that are sent out will be very complicated. Painstaking effort is needed to figure them out. If different "need messages" get crossed, that is when calamity occurs.

Crossed messages can be explained on two levels:

A. Internal Message Chaos

The messages from the spiritual body, mental body, and physical body have all been muddled. When the true order of influence is unchanged, the spiritual body guides the mental body, the mental body in turn guides the physical body, and the entire human body is at peace. All actions and behaviors are balanced, moral, and wise, indicating a healthy condition. But when the order of influence is distorted, the entire body will be sick and at war with itself. The resulting actions will be immoral and foolish. Because both the spiritual and mental bodies are confined within the physical body, and because the physical body is limited by space and time, the instincts of the physical body are playing most visible roles. This is so even at the evolutionary level of the Sage; egos still remain.

The physical body, with its instincts and limitations, loses its influence at the higher stages of evolution. When an individual cannot be limited by time, he will be called Transformed Immortal. When an individual cannot be limited by space, he will be called Terrestrial Immortal. When an individual cannot be limited by space or time, he will be called a Celestial Immortal, like God himself.

Eventually everyone, through continuing cultivation, will reach the highest evolutionary level. Taoism is the science that helps human beings reach this goal (explanations throughout and towards the end of this book; for further instructions please refer to *The Great Tao*). Lao Tzu assures us with these words: "The tree which fills the arms grows from the tiniest sprout; a tower of nine stories rises from a small heap of earth; the journey of a thousand miles commences with a single step."

B. Intercourse Chaos

When messages between or among people have been muddled, various problems arise. Human beings live within the confines of space and time, so every individual's thinking, embellished with unique interests and styles, is as varied as people's looks. Each has his own interests and unique style. No one, then, can completely avoid conflicts; someone has to be injured. But nobody is able to predict what is to be. To help us know, Sage Kuei Ku described five critical conditions under which human beings operate:

The Tao of Intercommunication

1. ILLNESS

The mighty can be disabled by disease. There is no life that can escape disease entirely. Illness can be regarded as a lesson to be learned by a particular individual; eventually it may be seen as a stimulant. But in most cases, it reduces an individual's capabilities, especially when it is chronic, when talent is always crippled.

2. FEAR

Fear and enmity always come together. By natural disasters or accidents, by deadly enemies or small insects, human life can be ended at any moment. In order to stay safe, one must be alert. Though fear is an accumulation of alertness, it can also be psychologically crippling. As King Solomon said, "The slothful *man* saith, *There is* a lion without, I shall be slain in the streets."

3. WORRY

The possibility of losing benefits or profits can cause people to worry to death. The potential of getting food, clothing, housing, position, fame, or entertainment can worry people sick. Worry and nervousness always come hand in hand.

4. ANGER

Frustration produces anger, and anger produces impulsiveness. Impulsiveness produces mistakes, and mistakes produce more frustration. Anger, stress and tension come together.

5. JOY

Yang Tzu (or Yang, Chu [600 B.C.–], a philosopher who advocated extreme selfishness—that is, to think of nothing but one's own gain) said, "Suppose a person lives a certain number of years. His childhood and old age takes about half his lifetime away. Then sleep at night and rest during the day takes the remaining half away. Then sickness, sorrow, affliction, confusion, and fear take the remaining half away. He has almost no time left for joy!" But Lao Tzu said, "The moment people open their hearts to happiness, sorrow has already followed in." Because joy relaxes people's defenses, pleasure and carelessness replace carefulness. Great sorrow will then sneak in like a thief.

With few exceptions, the multitude of this world suffers from the above Five Weaknesses of Human Nature. Some people will take advantage of these weaknesses to manipulate others (for example, one of two lovers claims to have a headache just before bedtime—a frequently used excuse). But a leader will know how to recast this as a weapon to conquer whoever needs to be conquered, including themselves.

For example, Yellow Stone Sage said, "A leader must know how to utilize his anger properly. Sometimes anger is the only power that gets things done."

At other times, anger needs to be dissolved out of angry people. Countless examples of this can be found in history or an individual's library of experiences, but one example emerges for its many sharp messages, namely, the story of a woman who was accused of adultery and who was brought to Jesus by an angry mob. In John 8:3-11, the angry mob taunted Jesus by asking: "Now Moses in the law commended us that such should be stoned. But what sayest thou?" The implications of these words were great, for they confronted Jesus with a dilemma. If Jesus answered "Yes," the mob would say, "Did you not teach love and save? How could you let her be stoned? You are a hypocrite." If he answered "No," the mob would accuse him of betraying the Law of Moses, and stone him too. It was a critical time indeed for Jesus, but he calmly stooped down and wrote on the ground with his finger. I suspect he was writing the words "sin," "liar," etc. And when they continued to ask him "he lifted up himself, and said unto them, He that is without sin among you, let him first cast a stone at her." He checked the mob with the same dilemma. But first he stooped down—an act displaying humility, quietude, silence, coolness, etc.—and diminished the mob's angry energy without violence. Then he kept writing on the ground words that may have reminded the mob of its own sins. Finally he stood up and told them that the pure among them may cast the first stone. Those words not only prevented him from breaking the Law of Moses and his own teachings, but also forced the mob to choose between proving its purity or hypocrisy. The only choice left was for the mob to scatter. The elders probably left first followed by the youngsters, who were, of course, less scheming. Jesus did not condemn the woman but sent her away telling her not to sin again. A skillful communicator can send clear and powerful messages through the use of verbal and nonverbal languages to hit the nails of human weaknesses right on the head.

    Human beings are very complicated creatures indeed. In the above case, most of the messages that were sent out were verbal—only a small portion was expressed by body action or movement. This is considered to be a relatively simple case, and is rarely found in the practical world, since human messages are infrequently delivered through direct speech. In most cases, the true meaning must be interpreted. Human beings seem to enjoy their own interpretive abilities.

II. INTERPRETATION

A story was handed down from long ago about a Buddhist monk who owned a very small temple and lived a very poor, unrecognized life with two disciples.

One day the disciples said to the monk, "Master, are you not getting tired of this kind of life? Why can't we become rich and famous like the other monks?" The master agreed and asked, "Do you have any ideas?" The clever disciples explained their idea and again the monk agreed. Immediately, the disciples began a publicity campaign, telling all the villagers that a certain Bodhisattva appeared and made their master psychic and that their master would be kind and generous enough to share his enlightenment with others and to guide those who seek help.

At first, only a few people came to seek guidance. But when these people testified to the monk's accuracy, more and more people came, and the monks became rich and famous. They rebuilt their temple, attracting even more people and money. In the consultation room, they installed a throne-like chair for the master, so that he sat regally like a Buddha. On both sides of the master stood the two disciples, who signaled to their master the things to say.

The disciples did quite a bit of detective work on the people who made appointments to see the master. Among the three of them, certain codes were devised to help the master recall forgotten information. If a question came up that they were unable to research, they would use arbitrary words from the Sutra and thereby get by.

The Tao of Intercommunication

One day, when the disciples were out doing some investigative work for the next appointment, a herald suddenly appeared and announced that the governor had arrived and wanted immediately to consult privately with the monk. The monk had no choice but to agree.

The governor came in, and, after exchanging the proper salutations with the monk, seated himself across from the monk on the other side of the room. The governor asked his first question: How safe was his position?

The monk absolutely did not know and, terribly anxious for his disciples' return, kept looking to his right and left sides for them. He was unable to utter one word.

The governor, at first confused, then nodded as if he understood. He went on to his second question: Was he going to be promoted?

The monk, in a panic, looked up at the ceiling as if to say, "How in heaven's name would I know?" Then he looked down, still unable to utter a word.

But the governor nodded his head again. He went on to his third question: How much success would he have if he declared independence from the central government?

At this point, the monk was so nervous he could do nothing but cover his ears with his hands and shake his head, crying, "I do not know! I do not know!" He became so hysterical he passed out.

The governor stood up, bowed, and left the room. When his counselors asked him how he felt about the consultation, the governor replied, "The monk is like God! He answered every question I had long harbored. He saved my life!" Because of these comments, the monk became even more famous.

Why was the governor so pleased?

Although he did not realize it, every answer came from his own interpretations, not from the monk. He interpreted the first "answer" to mean "Be careful.... Look around you.... Someone is waiting to do you harm." The second "answer" was interpreted to mean "Everything is in your favor. Your are definitely going to get a promotion." The third "answer," the covering of the ears and shaking of the head, was interpreted to mean that his proposal was against the law, that it must never be carried out. The cries of ignorance and fainting were thought to be attempts at cutting him off to protect him from saying anything more incriminating in case he was overheard.

Interpretation is an art people truly relish indulging in. Everyday, everywhere, there are millions of "governors" interpreting everything that happens around them, hardly minding whether their interpretations are correct or not. Enormous numbers of people are enjoying themselves thus from the moment the sun rises each morning.

In ancient China, the central government had a department specially set up to interpret God's (universal) will. Whenever there was an earthquake, tornado, flood, drought, locust invasion, etc., the department would issue its interpretation of how the heavens wanted the administration to improve its policies. The department also measured the accuracy of its interpretations after its suggestions were implemented. The interpretations usually helped promote good policies for the people.

Of all the methods used in interpreting universal will, I-Ching is probably the most accurate mathematical method to emerge in human history (refer to *The Great Tao*, Chapter 8). Because it is so logical and rational, it is almost second nature for those who wish to be successful to use it as an adviser.

Now we must return to our subject, interpretation, which is most necessary and vital to human survival. As Sage Kuei Ku explained, "An insect flying may mean life or death to an organization." Four procedures are involved in interpretation. According to Sage Kuei Ku, they are as follows:

The Tao of Intercommunication

A. Essence of Movement

The interpreter must be a person who is extremely still, calm, quiet, circumspect, and extremely knowledgeable of history. According to the theories of Yin and Yang, only the still can catch every motion, only the inactive can overtake the action, and only the motionless can distill the essence of movement. Behind anything that moves in the universe, there must be a reason or cause, for movement is the effect. Stillness and movement, cause and effect—these are the four instruments of an interpreter.

B. Picturing

After the essence of movement has been caught, the interpreter must begin to draw a "picture." Sage Kuei Ku called it "image." This "picture" could be a landscape, map, statistical chart, a "scratch of likeness" (of a criminal, etc.), and so on. Sometimes this "picture" can be just a story, fable, or parable. Then the interpreter must search into the past to try to find a similar or closely matching "picture." If such a match can be found, which is very likely, the facts or history behind the match will be the meaning of the new "picture." For example, if a certain movement is developing, and an expert interpreter takes its essence and places it on a chart, he can compare the chart to a similar one that was formed forty years ago and know that the same results will occur for the present case. If, instead, the new "picture" is an independent phenomenon, the interpreter has to compose new rationale to explain it.

C. Evidence

No matter what category the "picture" belongs to, the interpreter is obligated to collect as much information or evidence as possible to support whatever the meaning of the interpretation will be. Also, the interpreter is responsible for collecting as much counter evidence as possible.

D. Unmistaken Conclusion

Finally the interpreter will be able to present his conclusions, which will be his best possible interpretations, which in turn will contain the least percentage of mistakes.

Any interpretation could be clouded by the interpreter's subjectiveness. Hence, precautionary measures eliciting objectivity and calmness and coolness of mind are incorporated into the four procedures.

You may wonder why we must labor through such a difficult procedure and waste so much time and energy finding out the true meaning of a message sent out by others. Why not encourage everybody to use straight talk instead? We could ask everyone to put every card on the table in order to prevent interpretation mistakes; but no matter how clear straight talk will be, human beings will still try to interpret other meanings into it. Maybe it is a human language problem: the words leave too many blanks to fill. Even the most straightforward kinds of talk—that is, between superiors and subordinates, husbands and wives, and so on—must still be figured out. Sometimes too much explanation can aggravate a bad situation: the more words there are, the more interpretations there are.

A great leader, then, must say few words. His orders must be simple, short, and clear. And he must ask the listener to repeat the order to be sure the meanings understood are the same as the meanings given. No more, no less. Unfortunately, interpretation will never cease no matter what you do.

Let us examine the case of Mr. B., who was in middle management and who was living not far from his boss Mr. M., an Executive V. P. From time to time Mr. M. went over to Mr. B.'s house to have a drink and talk over matters. And Mr. B. was invited over to Mr. M.'s house occasionally. The increasing intimacy served both men well.

Suddenly Mr. B. detected some coldness from Mr. M. after his last visit to Mr. B.'s house. This made Mr. B. very uncomfortable. As hard as he tried he could not figure out what caused the change.

He then came to me for consultation. And we went over every detail, screened out the previous visits, and finally concentrated on the last visit to Mr. B.'s house. We reexamined everything that happened during the visit.

One "picture" showed Mr. B.'s wife calling Mr. B. from the other room as he and Mr. M. were talking. Mr. B. excused himself and left for the other room, talked to his wife for a little while, and then reappeared in the living room. Mr. M. said, "Well, I had better get going." Mr. B. immediately went to the front door and opened the door for Mr. M. and Mr. M. left.

This scene definitely raised some questions. Mr. M. may have interpreted that he was not welcome. Even worse, Mr. M. may have thought he was being thrown out of the house in a rude, unbearable, and insulting manner.

But Mr. B. and his wife were completely unaware they had done anything wrong. To Mr. B., he was only honoring Mr. M.'s wishes, showing his respect, and being polite by holding the door open. His wife called him away only to remind him of something before he forgot. And he did not ask Mr. M. to stay long because he thought Mr. M. was tired after a long day and needed to go home and rest. He was entirely unaware that two and two added together could mean something other than four to others.

Reminded of this Mr. B. felt terrible and wanted to go directly to Mr. M. to explain, but I stopped him from doing so because it might cause Mr. M. some embarrassment. The best solution was to ignore the entire episode and think of finding a better opportunity to restore the relationship. Fortunately the occasion came soon: Mr. M.'s daughter's birthday.

Mr. and Mrs. B. brought a nice gift from Mr. B.'s hometown to Mr. M.'s house. Then Mr. B. explained to Mr. M. that Mrs. B. had planned for this occasion a long time, that she had wanted to tell him (Mr. M.) that night he come over to their house, that after discussing it over they had decided to keep it a secret until his daughter's birthday, and that they had decided instead to bring the gift over personally to surprise his daughter. The explanation made Mr. M. very happy and subtly swept away the clouds of suspicion. Thereafter, the intimate relationship between them lasted a long time. Mr. B. was promoted continually.

III. PERSUASION

Persuasion is what induces others to believe, think, or do what someone wants. By definition persuasion (and subsequently any method of persuasion) is limited to influencing emotions and wills. In contrast the word "convince" is used to describe a method's action if it appeals to reason, rationale, and understanding. Finding a word that captures both sets of nuances is difficult. The three faculties of the mental body—thought (rationale), emotion, and will (decision making)—all work together and are inseparable, but there is no word that incorporates all of these meanings. For purposes of furthering understanding, the definition for the word "persuade" will include the definition for the word "convince." The word "convince" retains its original meaning and may be used interchangeably with "persuade," depending on the circumstances.

In an organization the leaders are responsible for clarifying missions, motivating working spirit, supervising work procedures, solving all kinds of problems, controlling workmanship and productivity, making decisions, and so on. In order to do all these well, leaders have to rely on their powers of persuasion every step of the way. If the organization is a powerful structure and the leaders are backed up by power, then leaders need only give orders in case any persuasion is needed. In such situations the leaders prevail over their subordinates, since the leaders are in a favored position. Preference of this nature makes work easier. But if the organization is structured so that power is equally distributed among the workers and leaders cannot give orders, then the only weapon leaders have left may be persuasion. So far, we have discussed two kinds of persuasive methods: prevailing orders and ordinary persuasion. Both will be discussed in detail in the paragraphs that follow.

Persuasion is not solely used by leaders on workers; sometimes workers need to induce their leaders too. Since the privilege of making the final decision often belongs to the boss, persuasion from subordinates is often presented in the form of suggestions. A good suggestion may concern the well-being of many people. Sometimes it concerns matters of life and death. How bosses may be persuaded to accept a suggestion will be another focus of this chapter.

A. Order

When leaders in favored positions to prevail over subordinates use verbal, nonverbal, or written means to issue orders, the receivers must execute the order in accordance with the contents of the order, under normal circumstances. Why must orders be executed?

The Tao of Intercommunication

1. RULE OF ORDERS

Three rules make the orders executable:

a. Do as I say; you will be rewarded.

b. Do as I say; if you disobey, you will be punished.

c. Do as I say because it is legal, reasonable, or rational to do so. This must be supplemented by passion or emotion on the part of the subordinates. If rapport has been established between a leader and his followers (because of patriotism, love felt by subordinates for their leader, feelings of obligation towards him, and so on) they will do anything—even die—for him.

In all cases, order and power goes hand in hand. To ensure that an order is executed fully, the leader must have or be backed up by enough power. Otherwise, how will he reward subordinates for jobs well-done? How will he punish those who disobey him? Even though subordinates may sympathize with their leader, or know he is right in their hearts, they will not obey him if they cannot derive advantages from obeying, nor will they obey if they know they cannot be punished. When they see a lack of power, they will place themselves in a "wait and see" position. Then the leader will be stranded.

In 1899, the young Emperor Kuan-Hsu was watching his empire crumble. Narcotics (opium) were smuggled incessantly into every corner of the country. Crime was rampant. The trade and national deficits were astronomical. The entire government was overwhelmed by bureacracy, idlers, extravagance, and waste. Almost every official was involved in some form of scandal or corruption. The economy and industries fell into extreme difficulties. The entire country was in an incompetitive situation, and at the root of all the problems was government incompetence. Emperor Kuan-Hsu tried to reform the government and the system by issuing enormous numbers of imperial orders. At times one hundred imperial orders were issued in a day. One hundred days later, he was imprisoned, ending what was to be called by historians the Hundred-Day Reformation. Later he was poisoned to death at thirty-six years of age. Though he had the empty title of Emperor, he had no power, so none of his imperial orders was executed. But his defeat did change the entire history of China. Three years later after his death came the revolutionary downfall of the Dynasty. Otherwise, the present-day government would be similar to those of Britain or Japan.

As you can see, the emperor meant well, but everything he did went against the three rules. Consequently his orders were worthless. He could have gone along with the old powers and waited for more favorable timing. Or he could have became one of the corrupt to ensure his survival. But he chose none of these; he chose a very short-lived alternative. He would do what an emperor should do, regardless of success or defeat. Perhaps deep in his heart he knew he was doomed for defeat. But at least he won a favorable name in history. Indeed he did win the sympathy of the people and by his defeat provide the strongest cause for a revolution. And his new ideas for the country were completely implemented later. If this interpretation is true, the emperor was an intelligent, talented, and extremely wise man. He purposely defied the rules to issue orders even though he knew none would be executed in his time. Nevertheless, rules are rules, and nobody can change them, not even an emperor.

2. FORBIDDENS

Yellow Stone Sage provided us with two Forbiddens. Whoever defies them is inviting trouble for him- or herself.

a. Never issue many orders at one period in time. Many orders equal no order. As Lao Tzu said, "Too many laws (regulations) equal no law. One accomplishes nothing, yet confusion and expenses mount."

b. Later orders shall never contradict earlier orders.

No matter how powerful the order issuer is, if either of the above rules is broken, his power will automatically be canceled.

B. Ordinary Persuasion

In this case, the persuader has no special privilege or favored position that enables him to prevail over people. Worse, he may be in an unfavorable (even critical) position because he is trying to convince a client, customer, student, patient, subordinate, co-worker, stranger (or other people whom he knows little or nothing about) to accept or follow or even adopt his thinking, belief, behavior, actions, etc. Convincing others is an inescapable fact of life. Everybody is subject to this challenge. Actually, unknowingly, everyone practices persuasion in daily living. The only difference is some become achievers at persuasion; others, losers.

Persuasiveness and impressiveness go hand in hand. In most cases, the first impression may decide the outcome of

The Tao of Intercommunication

Expression	Excellent	Fair	Poor
Natural			
Serious			
Optimistic			
Generous			
Polite			
Broad-minded			
Charitable			
Considerate			
Clean-cut			
Understanding			
Credible			
Alert			
Warm			
Amicable			
Tender			
Honest			
Tolerant			

Expression	Excellent	Fair	Poor
Neat			
Clean			
Healthy			
Clothing			
Responsive			
Calm			
Outstanding			
Dependable			
Straightforward			
Diplomatic			
Accommodating			
Imposing			
Knowing			
Competent			
Courageous			
Giving			
Extolling			

Table 9.1

the entire situation. On the opposite page is a checklist for impressiveness. It is suggested that you check yourself objectively against each item on the list in order to gain a fair impression of your own impressiveness.

The list is much more than a test; it should serve as a guideline for self-improvement. According to the Sages, when people sincerely cultivate their own expression long and well enough, they will gradually develop a kind of charm and vigor that is indescribable, indisputable, even powerful. This is what is called charisma. Sometimes, when people see that charisma they are already convinced.

After a persuader establishes his impressiveness, the next area of emphasis will be verbal communication—that is, the use of language to deliver a particular message in order to persuade or convince others. This may be the highest art or technique of the human kingdom. A better part of the book *Kuei Ku Tzu* is devoted to this topic, which will be discussed in the next seven sections.

1. CONFIDENCE

Before you try to persuade others, regardless of the circumstances, your number one priority is to be perfectly confident. This confidence does not come from pure faith or hope; it is based on solid concepts and techniques. Our solid concepts are the theories of Yin and Yang, which have been thoroughly discussed in the second chapter. From those we know that nothing is absolute in the universe. As the Sage said, "Even the hardest wood has joints; the iron rock, its cleavage; the most intimate friendship, its chasm." Nothing is unbreakable; so one inevitable question arises: What is the right tool to use? Everything is negotiable; so another question is: How to negotiate? The students who took Sage Kuei Ku's final examinations knew they were typical confidence-training sessions (refer back to Chapter 2). The Sage said, "If you have no doubt, you have no fear. And you have confidence." Next, we shall discuss the solid techniques.

2. REFLEX

In order to persuade your opponent, let him persuade you first. Explained the Sage, "Whosoever opens his mouth, information will be obtained." Even though you may have already gathered all needed information from other sources, inducing people to speak up is still a priority. There are seven ways to elicit speech to gather information:

a. Asking questions.

b. Making up a story. People will follow suit.

c. Reconfirming people's stories. Purposely refute one or two points of the contents. Then check their responses.

d. On different occasions, repeat the same question.

e. Certain superstitious paths can be tread for information.

f. Pretending to be angry, hostile, or joyful. People will act accordingly.

g. Carefully watch people's tiny movements (eyes, body, hands—all can speak).

Then, carefully interpret: 1) what kind of people you are dealing with, and 2) what will be their advantages and disadvantages. Now, it should be your turn to speak.

3. CLASSIFICATIONS OF PEOPLE

The purpose is to determine what kinds of language are used by what kinds of people. Otherwise, you may be speaking to a wall. There are many ways to classify people:

a. Personality

According to the Five-Star System, people are categorized into five basic types. Every personality type has his own language (refer to Chapter 5).

b. Background

i. "To those who are educated, you shall say something comprehensive or profound," said the Sage.

ii. "To those who are erudite, you shall say something distinguished or analytical."

iii. "To those who are eloquent, you shall give only synopses or key points."

iv. "To those who are noble or of high status, you shall say something that increases strength or security."

v. "To those who are rich, you shall say something implying status or luxury."

vi. "To those who are poor, you shall say something that brings profit or benefit."

vii. "To those who are of low status, you shall say something humble or modest."

viii. "To those who are bold or intrepid, you shall say something brave or resourceful."

ix. "To those who are slow and unlearned, you shall say something sharp or clever."

x. "To those who are in doubt, you shall say something implying secrecy or specialness."

xi. "To those who are superiors, you shall say something of special or strategic effectiveness."

xii. "To those who are subordinates, you shall say something implying personal interests or private gains."

c. Dislikes

i. "Never speak of money directly to the faces of those who see themselves as very moral, loving, or spiritual. But you may speak of charity," said the Sage.

ii. "Never speak of difficulties before those who see themselves as courageous and powerful. But you may speak of duty."

iii. "Never speak of inadequacy before those who see themselves as intelligent. But you may speak of strategy."

iv. "Never speak perfunctorily before those who see themselves as intimate."

v. "Never speak confidentially before a stranger."

vi. "Never play a lute before a bull." (It is extremely dangerous to say the wrong things to the wrong person.)

In general, do not be too anxious to speak, because once you do speak, someone will always be convinced. When wood is piled up, the dry wood will light up first. When water is poured, the moist earth absorbs moisture easier.

Persuasion is difficult to master, but for "those who know how, there is nothing more fortunate in all the world." Continued the Sage, "First is a complete plan—no detail is left out. Second is perfect persuasion—no one resists. Third is total success—no one obstructs. But if the people you must persuade are difficult to classify or are difficult to convince, then the Principles of Advantage and Disadvantage shall be utilized."

4. PRINCIPLES OF ADVANTAGE AND DISADVANTAGE

All human beings have basic needs—the need to protect advantages and the need to avoid disadvantages. Advantage means any person, event, or matter that is supposed to be good or needed for one's best interests. Advantage also has spiritual, mental, or physical efficacy. Disadvantage means exactly the opposite. The two of them together make up an Yin-Yang pair.

Human nature basically loves advantage and hates disadvantage according to the following rules:

Love		Hate
Advantages	<—>	Disadvantages
Advantages	>	Advantages
Disadvantages	<	Disadvantages

Rule 1: In the case of a choice between advantage and disadvantage, people grasp advantage and shun disadvantage.

Rule 2: In the case of a choice between advantage and advantage, people weigh the advantages and grasp what is comparatively worthier.

Rule 3: In the case of a choice between disadvantage and disadvantage, people weigh the disadvantages and grasp what is comparatively less harmful.

Both Rules 2 and 3 are based on the theories of Psycho-Dynamics (refer back to Chapter 6). For the persuasion of people, regardless of who they are or what the surrounding circumstances are, no other method exists beyond the method derived from these three rules. The only questions left are how these rules may be presented to the persuadees and how maximum results may be obtained.

According to the Sage, people will immediately grasp what they need to grasp, and shun what they need to shun. Difficulties arise when people are unclear about what they should or should not grasp.

In such instances, the presence of a persuader who can effectively show people what is advantageous and disadvantageous is welcomed. Often that which is hidden is easily uncovered. The unfailing techniques, called *Hsiang-Pi*, and skills taught by the Sage for these purposes are explained below.

a. Hsiang

Hsiang means "image." As described earlier, the significance of images is the same as that of pictures, but the latter, as the saying goes, has the value of a thousand words. If something can be described as clearly as a picture, the resultant picture will definitely be projected into the targeted minds, and what is projected is what is seen, enabling an understanding of the advantage.

b. Pi

Pi means "comparison." Without comparison, the principles of Yin and Yang would not exist. There would also be no good or bad, advantage or disadvantage, greater advantage or lesser advantage, greater disadvantage or lesser disadvantage. These subtleties of comparison are often very confusing for most people. It is said that one hint is enough for the wise man, but most people are not always so wise, especially when they are deeply involved, for their lack of detachment and objectiveness muddle their view. Often an onlooker will have a clearer view because his detached and, therefore, clear mind will be able to grasp what is truly happening.

c. Skills

The persuader often is someone who is trained to be clear-headed, to think objectively, and be detached. He will analyze and explain all the good and bad points. Once the advantages and disadvantages are highlighted, the entire picture will be completely clear. Then those involved may naturally proceed to grasp the advantages. As the Sage said, "The moment the persuader clarifies the picture, the moment people are convinced. The fish knows nothing of the hook hidden within the bait. The convinced know not how they are convinced." The Sage described the persuader as drawing upon the following skills:

i. Calmness—presenting reasons, rationale, etc.

ii. Justice—presenting what something should and must be. People will listen.

iii. Happiness—presenting happy results. For example, "You will feel great if you. . . ."

iv. Anger—scolding, reproaching people to make them feel guilty.

v. Reputation—using famous people to encourage trust: "Mr. Famous is sponsoring . . . you should. . . ."

vi. Role model—using examples set by others: "Your father paid taxes, so you. . . ."

vii. Faith—presenting hope.

viii. Thriftiness—presenting economical arguments: "If you buy this bond, you can earn...."

ix. Profit—presenting gains to convince many to take risks.

x. Humility—presenting a pitiful image to win sympathy.

I can testify to the power of persuasion. After having worked hard in secondary school, I was accepted by the top university in the country. Because I was overjoyed, carelessness set in and I spent a part of my freshman year being deeply involved in a theatrical club. My involvement was so deep I neglected my studies, but, as a result, I produced a play, which was a success. I would always be proud of the fact that the president of the university attended the play and gave it good reviews.

But two people, whom I had personally invited, did not come. They were my secondary school teacher and her husband, whom I had invited out of love and respect for their honor, for they were very close to me. Their absence was very disappointing to me.

The next day I received a specially delivered letter from my teacher. I expected it to be congratulatory or apologetic, but it was neither. In the letter she reprimanded me for throwing away a valuable education for a silly indulgence. I felt very hurt, insulted, and angry. But I knew there was truth to the words.

I went to see her and her husband the next day to apologize. She explained they did not mean to diminish my proudest moment, that they had only the best intentions in their hearts for me. All of us were greatly moved, and tears welled in our eyes.

Returning back to school I immediately quit the club and buried myself in my studies.

In retrospect, the skills used by my teacher, the second and fourth skills, were very effective at persuading me to reevaluate my situation.

5. PRESENTATION

In persuasion, as in decision making, all the preliminary steps must be combined in a composition. In this case, the three rules, two techniques, and ten skills are combined in a composition consisting of four sections (also explained earlier in the previous chapter).

Both logical induction and deduction are represented by syllogisms, which are composed of a major premise, minor premise, and conclusion. For example:

	Major Premise:	Minor Premise:	Conclusion:
Induction:	Dogs and cats are animals	Dogs and cats are intelligent	Therefore, animals are intelligent
Deduction:	Human beings must die	Jesus was human	Therefore, Jesus died

The Tao of Intercommunication

Generally, logical induction and deduction are used in speeches, and the results are usually unspectacular. Usually the audience will take frequent breaks to get refreshed, fall asleep, or thin out and leave the auditorium half-empty. To counteract this, Taoist scholars prefer to use another form of logic in speech and writing, called Quaternary Logic. It is composed of a General Premise, Major Premise, Anti-Premise, and Conclusion. For example:

General Premise:	Major Premise:	Anti- Premise:	Conclusion:
Human beings must die	Jesus was human	But Jesus was also God	Therefore, Jesus died but was resurrected

According to deductive logic, Jesus is dead. But the entire basis for Christianity is that Jesus is not dead, that he is the savior who saves people because he himself is not dead. If Jesus is dead, how can he save others when he cannot even save himself? If this is so, Christianity cannot be established logically. But according to Taoist logic, Christianity can be established logically and perfectly, as exemplified above.

Whenever a theme needs to be established, it must be composed in four steps. The first step is to establish a general premise about a universal truth or any other topic you want discussed. Usually it is a commonly believed principle. The second step is to establish a major premise, your main thesis or point, idea, suggestion, etc. and its proof. The third step is to establish an anti-premise, which can be one or more theses that differs from or opposes the major premise and their proofs or disproofs. The final step is to establish a conclusion, which is essentially a synthesis. Almost nobody in the world can oppose it.

An example of this procedure can be as follows: The statement *Human beings must die* is a universal truth, proven repeatedly and without fail by countless cases. *Jesus was a man* is an important point presented as the major premise. History provides the proof for this proposition. *Jesus is a witch* is a possible anti-premise. So is *Jesus is a vampire*. But these are easily proven wrong. Only *Jesus was also God* is supported by numerous statements in the New Testament. Because he is the son of God, he shall not die. The conclusion: *Jesus died but was resurrected*. Without this logic, there would be no logical basis for Christianity.

Taoist Quaternary Logic consists of both syllogisms and dialectics. The persuasive power arising from such a combination can be incredible, whether presented in written or verbal form.

I have spoken to large and small audiences, professionals and laymen throughout many parts of the world countless times. I can testify that whenever I use Quaternary Logic in my speech, I receive tremendous response and credit. For example, I was invited to lecture at the University of Oregon. The program started at seven in the evening and was to last until ten. There were three speakers, and each was given one hour to speak. During the first hour only eight people were counted in the big auditorium. The second speaker took the precaution of advertising in the local newspaper and on television. But during the second hour only twelve people were counted in the auditorium. I started at nine. Suddenly the entire auditorium was filled to capacity. One hour passed, but the audience asked me to continue for another hour. Another hour passed, and I was asked to speak some more. This went on until twelve midnight. But nobody wanted to leave! Finally the coordinator had to ask people to leave. When that failed, he started pushing people away so that I could leave. I left the campus at one in the morning.

Another time I was invited to lecture at the University of Oslo in Norway. Every Wednesday night the university opened its great auditorium to the public to present hour-long educational programs of interest to the public. The university asked me to be a guest speaker at one of these night programs in addition to my regular schedule. I agreed. The coordinator told me that audiences at these programs were usually very small, hardly exceeding twenty people in an auditorium with seven hundred seats.

On the day I was to speak, as we drove up the great boulevard in front of the royal palace, we could see the campus plaza, where a large crowd had gathered in front of a huge building. It was around six in the evening. After parking the car, we walked toward the plaza and the building, which was the auditorium.

When the doors to the auditorium were opened, the inside was seen to be jam-packed with people. People were sitting in the aisles, stairs, floor, anywhere where space was available. And outside a crowd was still trying to get in. Then the guards were called to shut the doors, turn away those who could not get in, and collect money. It took them an hour and a half to do the work.

I started to speak at seven-thirty. One hour soon passed, but the audience refused to leave. People were crying out that they were willing to pay for another hour's lecture. But the university was caught in a dilemma: it was unable to collect money and it could not ask me to continue to speak. Nevertheless, I agreed to speak some more. Another hour passed, and then another. Still the audience refused to leave. This situation lasted until it was eleven-thirty.

Then the coordinator announced that the lecture would end in ten minutes. But when it did end, the audience crowded around on stage to ask questions and shake hands with me. I did not leave the campus until 12:30 a.m.

6. FURTHER TECHNIQUES

Finally, a few more words on persuasion have been left by the Sage:

a. Never persuade in a bad atmosphere.

b. Never persuade in an untimely manner.

c. Never persuade without persuading yourself first.

C. Suggestion

The persuader who has a good idea and occupies a position as a subordinate has the responsibility of persuading the superior, but he has no power to push the superior, as only the superior has the power to make the final decision to accept or reject the suggestion, even though the suggestion may be absolutely essential and expedient.

In this case the persuader has to be especially considerate of the superior's ego. If a good suggestion is accepted, it can help everybody—the superior, organization, and the persuader himself—win. If a good suggestion is rejected everybody loses, but the persuader himself is in most danger. A leader who cannot accept good suggestions is either foolish or egotistic. Egotism can make a person mean and cruel, especially in a case where the leader apparently knows the suggestion is wonderful and purposely puts it down. Under these circumstances, the persuader must be extremely cautious. He should either stay still and quiet or leave; otherwise, he is inviting trouble.

Besides the teachings in sections A and B of the latter half of this chapter, another practical technique for dissolving the superior's ego may be utilized. Dissolving the ego is difficult, because you cannot go to the superior and tell him to put aside his ego and listen to you—that would intensify his ego even more. The best solution, then, is to satisfy his ego on the one hand (always count in egotism as a part of consideration) and present the suggestions on the other hand.

In addition, it is suggested that you submit three plans at the same time whenever you are submitting any suggestions to your superior. One plan is the formal plan, the other two are alternatives. Such a presentation contains an important message to the superior: "You are the superior." Also tell him: "I have considered every possible point. Nothing has been left unconsidered for your convenience, Sir." This message tells him you are his useful and loyal subordinate; therefore, he has no reason not to accept your suggestion to make everybody a winner. In other words, if you want to dissolve the superior's ego, your own must be dissolved first.

An egotistic subordinate will make the superior extremely uncomfortable. A subordinate who is egotistic and strongly ambitious will push a superior into a defensive position. A defensive superior doubts everything the subordinate does or says. At least he must set aside a bit of time to figure out the subordinate's true intentions. The more that subordinate pushes, the more disquieted the superior becomes. Finally everyone will be a loser. The biggest loser, of course, will be the egotistic and ambitious subordinate. Please check to see how many people fitting this description are losers. They blame everybody but themselves, when they themselves are the actual causes of loss.

Not everyone is born a king. If you do not have the wisdom to serve your superior, even though you need his trust and help, you will not get a chance to climb up. You will definitely be finished in the first few steps. Mencius called those who are unwilling "organizational insulators standing in a dead end."

Since most people have to pass through the stages of being subordinates, it is very important that they be beloved subordinates. The Sage provided three Yin-Yang pairs along with further suggestions for admirable and effective conduct to help a subordinate earn his superior's appreciation:

1. YIN-YANG PAIRS FOR EFFECTIVE CONDUCT

a. Your outstanding background, morality, talent, etc. will make your superior admire you.

b. Secretly doing favors for the superior to make him like you.

c. Solving problems to make the superior rely on you.

d. Secretly covering up the shortcomings of the superior to make him grateful to you.

e. Clearly saying "Yes" or "No." Every yes or no must be supported by good reasons so the superior will respect you.

f. Keep secrets to make the superior fear you.

If you can persuade the superior to appreciate you, you can persuade him to accept any good suggestion of yours. Finally everybody will be winners.

2. EFFECTIVE CONDUCT BEFORE THE SUPERIOR

When speaking before your superior, you must be mindful of the following:

a. Never quarrel.

b. Never joke.

c. Never be sophisticated.

d. Never break a promise.

e. Never satirize.

f. Never say anything that is forbidden or too sensitive to be mentioned.

g. Never leave unsaid what should be said.

h. Never speak in disorder.

The Tao of Intercommunication

i. Never equivocate or speak obscurely or ambiguously.

j. Never lecture.

All of these rules are not difficult to follow, but many people just do the opposite. "Therefore, people's failure started at the very beginning," said the Sage. Because of these simple oversights, many precious talents are wasted. People who care about their careers must know these rules. The earlier, the better. These precautions will guarantee the first step of achievement.

Intercommunication is not a privilege possessed solely by human beings, but in its use human beings can surely dominate over other organisms. All the successful leaders, from the beginning, were the ones who knew the Tao of Intercommunication and utilized the skills. These are not difficult to use, but most people just do the opposite. Lao Tzu said, "My words are very easy to know, and very easy to practice; but few in the world are able to know and practice them. . . . There is an original and all-comprehending principle in my words, and an Authoritative Law for the things which I enforce. It is because they do not know these that men do not know me. They who know me are few, and practice on my account will be greatly rewarded."

Since the world tends toward the opposite, let us see how the Sages can be privileged by true opposition. Lao Tzu described privilege as "that whereby the rivers and oceans are able to receive the homage and tribute of all the valley streams. Privilege is in placing themselves (rivers and oceans) lower than others (valley streams). It is thus that they are kings of them all. So the leader, wishing to be above men, puts himself by his words below them, and, wishing to be before them, places himself behind them."

"It is the TAO (WAY) of HEAVEN not to strive, and yet it skillfully overcomes; not to verbally speak, and it is skillful in (obtaining) the right response; does not summon, and yet people come to it of themselves. Its demonstrations are quiet, and yet its plans are skillful and effective."

Yen, Yin (approximately 600 B.C.) was the prime minister of the Kingdom of Chi and a very famous diplomat in ancient China. His administration made the kingdom strong and wealthy. One day when the driver of his carriage went home from work, his wife asked him for a divorce. She said to the driver, "His Excellency is an honorable prime minister, and the world knows his good name. I have found him to be very humble, never noisy or rude towards anyone. But you, only a driver, are so conceited and haughty. I have heard that you have been yelling with fury at everyone on the street. Now I realize that you are a nobody without a future. That is why I am divorcing you."

Shimomura, Kiyoshi was an active reporter working for Japan Daily Broadcasting Corporation. One day an order was received from headquarters promoting him to Chief Director Secretariat. Learning of this, he immediately sought the counsel of Takeda, Yutaka, who was the Executive Vice President of New Japan Steel. Before that Takeda was Director Secretariat of Fuji Steel and was honored as the premier secretary in Japan. In his first sentence to Shimomura, Takeda advised, "Please never be that driver of Yen, Yin."

Chapter 10

The Tao of Riches and Fame

One day a very large birthday party was held for a ninety-year-old man. Among those present to celebrate with and congratulate the man was Chuan Tzu. Chuan Tzu left the party in tears, for he knew the kind man was nearing his end.

I have heard that, especially in the business world, growth is emphasized. Everyone is proud of the word "growth." The bigger the growth, the better. Most are ashamed if their businesses are not growing fast enough. In some ways, the word "management" and the word "growth" go hand in hand. If the business has not grown month after month or year after year as expected, then management is the first to be blamed. People are willing to pay any price for a talented manager who has the magic that can make their business grow bigger and bigger. It seems the managers have done wonders: many organizations that are indeed "giants" are still growing.

The Tao of Riches and Fame

Suppose there is a person who is exceeding his ideal weight of 150 pounds, yet he keeps popping food, liquids, vitamins, etc. into his mouth. Pretty soon he weighs 350 pounds, but he is still growing. Then he develops high blood pressure, hardening of the arteries, angina, diabetes, kidney failure, and so on, but he brags he is in the care of a good doctor. I'll bet you know what advice a really good doctor will give him.

On the personal level, more and more people are becoming aware of the discipline of dieting—especially the practice of watching cholesterol levels—and the benefits it brings. Even business organizations, commendably, are helping their employees watch their weight. But on the organizational level, we rarely hear about a "weight watching" program. Strange, considering the enormity of the appetite for growth and the seriousness of the "weight" problem. I have often heard many organizations "complain" about their "high blood pressure," their "hardening arteries," etc. They seek and try, but to no avail, miracle formulas, never thinking that the best medicine is DIET. I admire the policies of a few European corporations. They are world-famous, but have kept themselves trim, and are therefore extremely healthy. I know from the bottom of my heart that they will be very healthy in the future. In Chapter 5, the Five-Star System awaits those who care.

Lao Tzu gave us this advice: "Knowing ignorance is strength. Ignoring knowledge is sickness. If one is sick of sickness, one is not sick.... Better to stop short than fill to the brim. Oversharpen the blade and the edge will soon blunt."

A famous parable told by Mencius is worth mentioning: "There was a man who grew vegetables in his field. He watched them closely day and night. But he thought they did not grow fast enough, so he tried pulling at every one of them to make them grow. He thought, 'Now they are taller.' The next day he went to the field and pulled at them some more. The third day, he found that all his vegetables had died."

The Tao of Riches and Fame

Beginning largely in the nineteenth century, human beings became more clever. All kinds of artificial methods have been used to encourage natural growth, so that two thirds of the resources on our planet are now used up, even as human population continues to grow. Industrial wastes (including chemicals and nuclear wastes) choke human, animal, marine, and plant life. Our topsoil is quickly disappearing. Our ozone is disappearing. Acid rain kills our oxygen producing forests, when they are not being chopped down. If we do not die from painful seizures due to toxins in our bodies, or die from suffocation or starvation, we will die by being burned alive by nuclear weapons. At the touch of a button, or a spark of mis-wiring, all that we have known or loved will be destroyed. For all the "help" civilization has received, we can thank one or two greedy and "clever" people.

Since one or two especially smart people invented the word "loan" in Europe, how many kings and lords became addicted to this "help" and exposed themselves and their subjects to the will of the banks? How many people have been driven into the snake pit of debt because of the words "tax deductible" and "credit"? How many corporations have been brought to their knees because of the word "depreciation"? Because of these or related words, human beings have been driven to bring the planet to the point it is now. None of these words need exist, if human beings were not greedy.

Human beings are the greediest creatures alive on this planet. Animals are greedy, but to an extent only slightly greater than plants. Animals have only physical and mental bodies, so they are not driven; plants have only physical bodies, so they are neither driven nor scheming. But when it comes to the human being, King Solomon said, "Everything is beautiful in its time but He [God] put spirit in man's mind." As the spirit is something that cannot be limited by space and time, its being confined in a limited vessel causes many problems to arise.

However, problems need not arise if human beings live in

accordance with the proper order of influence, by following the guidance of first the spiritual and then the mental bodies. They have everything to gain by doing so: they will evolve into the Divine Kingdom, or Kingdom of God. But if a human being lets the physical body take charge and lets the mental and spiritual bodies aid it, that entire being is a source of endless trouble. When this is the case, the first symptom that appears is greed.

Every good book in the world has taught people not to be greedy. Certain religions have even found it necessary to incorporate this teaching into their system of practice, such as, forcing its followers to lead an ascetic life. But an ascetic lifestyle just shows the strength of greed's drive; it shows how much the human being can endure—give up—to obtain what he wants. In some cases, an ascetic's greed may be stronger than anyone else's. Some political systems have even used extreme pressure to suppress human greed. So far, no philosophy, religion, or political system has succeeded.

People are greedy for many things: food, clothing, sex, money, power, status, fame, etc. Though these go by many names—including "economy," "security," "benefit," etc.—it all boils down to money. Since money's invention, it is the most wanted thing in a human being's heart, because it can buy anything a human being could want. According to an old saying in China, money can "make the devil turn the mill"—in other words, it can work miracles. Because it is so loved, how can anyone under heaven forbid people from loving it? Nevertheless, the universe has its rules for money lovers:

1) If you love money you will get it, but you have to sacrifice some aspect of your life.

2) You have the money you earn, but you do not really *hold* it. For example, if you put the money in a safe, or bury it underground, you do not hold it—the bank or soil has it. All you have are numbers. The more you love your money, the less you will actually *hold* it.

3) You truly hold your money when it is in your hand, being used. Money is essentially used by being spent. If you spend it in the wrong place, a great calamity will befall you.

4) If you have a lot of money and you do not spend it or share it with the proper people, somebody will spend it for you, in a way that pains you deeply. If no one is spending it, you may lose something important to you: your bodily organs, your loved ones, etc. (For details refer to *The Great Tao*, Chapter 8.)

Taoism explains the situation with money with two rules:

1) The above rules remain steadfast, except in one case. That exception is when money, power, status, etc. are heaven's rewards to an individual who has served it and accomplished his mission well. That individual can really enjoy his or her rewards because he or she has heaven's blessing.

The secret is to place your mission first. Everything else comes second. Your accomplishment of your mission is why you are here in the first place. Calamities arise because people put off or ignore their mission and chase after the secondary things. Jesus said, "Seek first His kingdom and His righteousness and all these things (things to eat, drink, and wear) shall be yours as well."

Taoism has never put down human needs. As a matter of fact, Lao Tzu emphasized that people should have fine food, beautiful clothes, comfortable carriages... enjoy their lives—if these are well deserved. It is only when people fall in love with these things, desire them more and more, accumulate them, store them and hide them, watch day and night over them, and search after them that they bring trouble upon themselves and others. Because you want them, others want them too. Because you accumulate them, others accumulate them too—by taking them away from you. That is why Lao Tzu said, "Amass a store of gold and jade and no one can protect it." From two little brothers who fight over a toy to two great countries that fight for basically the same thing, both the host and the thief are guilty of greed.

2) Everybody wants to be rich (materially and spiritually). But how rich is rich? It is a very relative concept. Let us use money as an example in explaining this concept. Not long ago there was a case of a woman who owed a man $50. The man threatened her to return his money, but she refused. One day he poured gasoline on her and burned her badly. Fortunately she was not killed and the authorities arrested the man. Then there was the case of a man who gambled away $1 million in a few minutes at a gambling casino. He just smiled and carried on as if nothing had happened; $1 million meant nothing to him. In one case, $50 was enough to kill for; in another case, $1 million meant nothing. Exactly how rich is rich? According to Lao Tzu, "The moment you say to yourself 'It is enough' is the moment you are rich." According to Yellow Stone Sage, "Nothing can be of greater happiness than when one feels contented. Nothing can invite more bitterness than when one desires more."

Our world has come to this point. The Great Tribulation is only one step away. Because we see it, we cannot pretend not to know, because ignoring knowledge is sickness. Knowing the mistakes people have made is our strength. We still have time to undo them. Let us reason with our greed.

In the new age of management, the premier duty is to reconsider carefully the true mission, and place profits second. Have these not brought us enough stress, suffering, and sickness? How much benefit have they really brought us anyway? Must the last and biggest "benefit" to us be total destruction? What about your evolution? Your children's evolution? So before you invent anything, check its side-effects first. Before you market anything, check its results first. Before you produce anything, check the quality first. Before you promote anything, check the benefits first.

But many of you may say your corporation is a profit-oriented organization, not a social service. Nobody wants you to lose; that is why Taoist scholars suggested two methods of perpetual gain. In one case, you can continue to gain and not lose everything if you place a limit on profit. In another case you are welcome to make as much profit as you like, but you should not feel guilty about it as long as you have a program of sharing profits with society and replacing the resources. Thus, your benefits and blessings will be everlasting.

One day Mencius arrived at the Kingdom of Liang. King Huei greeted him at the palace and said, "Honored Sir, I am truly grateful that you have traveled thousands of miles to visit our humble kingdom. I assume you bring good ideas to profit this kingdom?" The senior scholar replied, "Oh! Your Majesty. Pray never utter the word 'profit.' Only love and righteousness should leave the lips of Your Majesty. If your people, from high to low, fight each other strictly over profit, your kingdom shall be in great danger."

Your corporation needs you to revitalize it. Your country needs you to strengthen it. Your world needs you to save it. Billions of lives await you to protect them. The world's future is in your hands. Whichever direction you want it to go, it will go. Behold the Great Tribulation is at hand.

CONCLUSION

Here is a priceless gift which has been given to me. I will pass it onto you. According to historical records, a turtle rose from the Lo River 6,000 years ago. On his back was found a certain pattern,

Figure 10.1

Conclusion

which Taoist scholars have interpreted to be the following numbers:

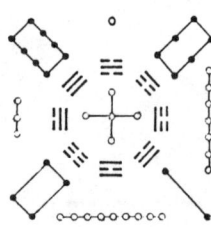

8	1	6
3	5	7
4	9	2

a. Pattern on Turtle b. Numbers in Magic Square

Figure 10.2a-b

The numbers came pre-arranged like those in a magic square, so that however one reads across the square and added up its numbers, one would obtain the number 15. If an octagon is superimposed on the square, a Magic Octagon or "Subtle Casket" is created:

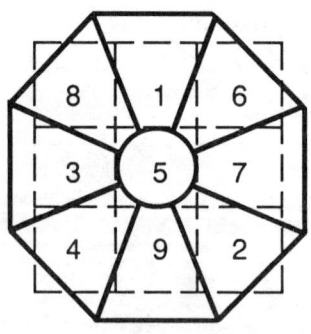

Figure 10.3

When the eight trigrams replace the numbers, the full meaning of Taoism is given.

CONCLUSION

Figure 10.4 Pa-Kua, Symbol of Taoism

The Subtle Casket actually harbors an enormous number of meanings and has a multitude of usages, so that it could be regarded to be as valuable as the treasures of Golconda. For example, you may use it as a blueprint for your practical work. On a personal level, the Eight Attitudes and the Eight Styles of Management can be found in the blueprint. On the organizational level, the locations of different departments may be found in the blueprint. Japanese corporations have only recently begun to pay more attention to the location of their corporate departments. Many companies have been finding 50 to 85 percent jumps in their productivity and ability to intercommunicate after arranging their departments according to this blueprint. My explanation is this arrangement allows for more convenient inter-departmental coordination. Their explanation is summed up by their naming the arrangement "The Study of Human Behavior Under the Influence of Electronic Waves." Many people indeed have recognized the blueprint's infinite power, a power that is not

Conclusion

limited by space or time. On the personal health level, position #1 on the blueprint reveals that corporate stress and tension can be reduced by the practice of Internal Exercises. Position #9 on the blueprint reveals how sex life may be used to increase business productivity and effectiveness. Health may also be optimized through proper diet (#8). (For examples please see Appendix.) How you use the blueprint depends on your own creativity and cultivation. This blueprint can be everything that will benefit you. Its potential is unlimited (for details please refer to *The Great Tao*).

Figure 10.5

North

6 Inspection Security (CEO) Organization Heaven Attitude Counsellor	1 Internal Exercises Conference Negotiation Finance Accounting Budget Water Attitude	8 General Affairs Balanced Diet Construction Worker Quality Control Factory Mountain Attitude
7 Consumption Recreation Entertainment Controlling Reception Lake Attitude	5 Board (Chairman) CEO Productivity Leadership Tao	3 New Employee Invention Staffing Research Development Board of Directors Thunder Attitude
2 Mastery Retreat Retirement Services Feedback Secretary Earth Attitude	9 General Business Marketing Advertising Sex-life Administration Fire Attitude	4 Promotion Training Education
Information Health-care Wind Attitude

South

Conclusion

•••••••••••••••••••••••••••

Finally, I would like to finish this book with an interesting story, since we started with a story. In the year 300 B.C., the central government of the great Chou Dynasty was fractured, and feudal lords were fighting each other for control of the empire. Eventually the empire was divided into seven kingdoms. The western-most Kingdom of Chin was ruled by Duke Shaw and was very weak. Extremely ashamed of this weakness, Duke Shaw started a publicity campaign to attract the help of talented men. The young man who came to apply for a position was to change the course of history. His name was Kung-Sun, Yang.

Kung-Sun, Yang began learning the many styles of management at a very young age, because he was very anxious to do great things for the world. Hearing that Premier Tien, Wen of the Wei Kingdom was a great man, Kung-Sun went to the kingdom to try to gain employment under the premier. When he arrived, Premier Tien had already died. The successor, Kungshu, Ts'o, interviewed Kung-Sun and immediately hired him. Premier Kungshu found his protege to be very dependable and extremely talented and planned to entrust him with an important position. Suddenly Premier Kungshu became very ill. The King of Wei personally came to see the premier and found that he was nearing his end. The King had no choice but to ask the premier to recommend a good successor to his position. Kungshu immediately recommended Kung-Sun highly.

But the King's only reply was, "That young man...."

The Premier realized the king was not going to use Kung-Sun, so he said, "Pray, Your Majesty, if you have decided not to use Kung-Sun, please kill him. Never let him leave this kingdom. His employment by another kingdom will be a great misfortune for you."

The King agreed. After a few comforting words he left.

Premier Kungshu immediately summoned Kung-Sun to tell him

CONCLUSION

what had transpired and to tell him to flee. He said, "My guiding principle is to be loyal to His Majesty first and be loyal to friends second. Please leave immediately!"

But Kung-Sun replied, "Please rest, Your Excellency. I do appreciate your mercy from the bottom of my heart, but I will not leave Wei. Because His Majesty has not taken the first good advice to use me, you may rest assured that His Majesty will not take the second advice to have me killed."

Kungshu soon died.

Later, the King refused a second appeal for Kung-Sun by his good friend Minister Prince Tung because he did not believe "that young man." Kung-Sun had no choice left but to leave for the Kingdom of Chin, where he knew a position may be found. There he met Minister Chin-Chien, who was in charge of Duke Shaw's recruitment effort. After interviewing Kung-Sun, the Minister found him skillful and immediately set up an interview with the Duke. But during the interview, Kung-Sun bored the Duke to sleep. The Minister was disappointed and blamed Kung-Sun for ruining the interview.

Kung-Sun explained, "But I was speaking of the highest level of management, the one implemented by Emperor Yao. Because I had no idea what level of management would be of interest to Duke Shaw, I dared not present myself with a level of learning that His Majesty may find to be inadequate. I will have no chance of reversing his opinion about me. Now that I am more knowledgeable of the situation, please be patient with me and set up another interview for me. I believe I will persuade him this time."

Another interview was set. Five days later, Kung-Sun went to see Duke Shaw again. This time he spoke of a level of management that was implemented by King Wu. But the Duke stopped him halfway and said, "Your memory is splendid, and your knowledge extensive as well. But Honored Sir, I do not see that we share the same viewpoint. I'm afraid we have no chance of working together."

Conclusion

Then he ordered Kung-Sun to retire.

Already knowing the results, the Minister met Kung-Sun outside the palace, and blamed him bitterly. But Kung-Sun smiled and said, "Now I know exactly what the Duke wants. . . ."

"Kung-Sun, put any thought out of your mind. You have already lost all your chances. I cannot be of help," cut in the Minister.

Kung-Sun continued, "Your Excellency, I appreciate what you have done for me already, putting up with me for so long. But this is not a small matter. If I leave now, history might blame you if you said you could not or would not help."

The Minister gave in saying, "Very well then, I will try again. But I cannot guarantee His Majesty will want to see you again. However, I will do my best."

Five days later, Duke Shaw summoned Kung-Sun and said to him, "What I really want is someone with some talent to make my kingdom wealthy and strong immediately. Sir, let no more time be wasted. If you know how to talk to me, speak! Otherwise, you had better seek a better place of work."

Kung-Sun replied, "Your Majesty is anxious to strengthen your esteemed kingdom. I do have the method for getting results immediately."

Kung-Sun explained his proposal, as the Duke listened with increasing interest: "My Lord, the management style that obtains fast results is completely different from those that I have mentioned previously. The aforementioned emphasizes talking and working with your subjects and loving and taking care of them. Though the democratic form of management produces results that are slow to show, the results are stable. The fastest way for management to get results is to practice the Legalist Style of Management. It is cruel and uncompassionate, and the people will loath it. But in bringing results it is fast and effective."

The Duke pulled out his sword and roared, "Why do people loathe it?!"

CONCLUSION

Kung-Sun calmly replied, "Your Majesty, when a lute becomes dissonant, one must tune it. Management reforms society when it is out of working order. When people become set in their ways of life, they are unwilling to change their ways. If we do not implement changes, we cannot correct the problems that cause weakness. But if we try to make changes, the people will reject it; the future welfare of the state will not enter their minds. Then we must fail in the end. My Lord, have you heard of Kuan, Chung, the Premier of the Kingdom of Chi? Two hundred years ago he changed every established system and turned the entire kingdom inside out. But the kingdom soon became the strongest and wealthiest kingdom under the sky."

"If you can do whatever Kuan, Chung could do, I will honor anything you say," the Duke replied.

Kung-Sun said, "My Lord, what Kuang did was first make the kingdom rich. A kingdom without wealth could not be strong. And in order to be strong and wealthy, one must depend on the people. They must be made to become more productive. And to make them more productive, one must order them to do what they might dislike doing. Then your order must be made to be honored as law. Those who obey the law will be rewarded; those who do not obey will be punished unyieldingly. It is cruel but you will have what you desire immediately."

The Duke smiled and said, "I love it! Now I know you are talented!"

"My immense gratitude for your kind words. But as I have mentioned a little while before, this style of management is so different you might think it awkward at first. Enforcing the law is definitely not easy. Without the right person, the style cannot be implemented. There are three important principles: first, find the right person; second, the right person must be completely trusted and supported by the lord; third, once the lord has come to trust and support this person, he cannot listen to others' criticism, otherwise

Conclusion

there can be no hope of success. Now, Your Majesty, would you please consider these three principles for three days. If you decide to accept it, I will submit a detailed plan." Kung-Sun saluted the Duke and retired from court.

Minister Chien received Kung-Sun and blamed him again for kindling the Duke's interest and then withholding information to blackmail him.

"Your Excellency," explained Kung-Sun, "you do not understand. The practice of this style of management is different. It requires strong will and determination. If His Majesty is determined, it can be done. If he lacks these qualities, there is no point in wasting time."

The second day, the Duke could not wait to hear the plan and summoned Kung-Sun. But Kung-Sun refused to appear, telling the messenger the following: "We have set up a three-day agreement. If we cannot keep this agreement, how can we keep our promises in the future?"

Early in the morning on the third day, the Duke sent a beautiful carriage to take Kung-Sun to the palace, where he was honored with a seat and offered an apology for all previous misunderstandings. After politely thanking the Duke, Kung-Sun presented his plan and listed all the changes that must be implemented, always analyzing each change carefully. The two men conversed for three days and three nights. The Duke was never once tired. Then the royal order was issued: Kung-Sun was assigned the position of Premier.

The new Premier began legislation of all new laws. At the same time he had a thirty-foot-long pole erected in a plaza at the southern part of the city. An officer was ordered to tell the people that whoever was able to move the pole to the northern part of the city would be awarded ten barriers of gold. A massive crowd gathered around the pole, but nobody dared move it. Then the award increased to fifty barriers of gold. Then one man thought to himself, "This kingdom has never enforced one law or regulation. I might as well move it,

CONCLUSION

since I have nothing to lose and the pole is easy to move anyway. Who knows? I might really get something." So he moved it. The Premier summoned the man, praised him personally and awarded him fifty barriers of gold. Hence, the entire kingdom understood that the new Premier kept his word.

Not too long afterwards, a new law bearing the signature-seal of the Duke was made public. Many people started to comment. Some said it was good. Some said it was bad. All the critics were arrested, sentenced and jailed. The Premier explained to the people that they had the right to obey, not criticize, the law. No criticism would be tolerated by the government, which would punish any offenders. Once, the Duke's son criticized the new law, and the Premier reported him to the Duke. As a result the prince's mentors, teacher, and professor were sentenced (the prince was not punished because the law forbade the punishment of royal members). At the same time, two senior ministers who privately criticized the law were fired immediately. Soon the entire kingdom obeyed the law carefully.

Then the government ordered a tax increase of 300 percent, forcing people to work day and night. Within a very short period of time, the kingdom became wealthy, wealthy enough to support an army and defend itself. A little while later, it was able to take an offensive stance.

In a campaign against the Kingdom of Wei, the Premier personally led the troops and attacked and defeated Wei's armies. Land, including that of his old friend Prince Tung, was added to the possessions of the Kingdom of Chin.

Within the Kingdom of Chin, a victory of another kind was achieved. There was no fear of theft or criminals. No one dared commit a crime, because if anyone did, he or she would be sentenced to the borderlands, to farm the wasteland and expand the national boundaries. If the sentenced still disobeyed, they were killed. Once seven hundred prisoners were killed in one day.

By these means the Kingdom of Chin became the strongest and

Conclusion

wealthiest kingdom, exceeding all other kingdoms. Envoys from other kingdoms arrived continuously, bearing gifts or deeds to land.

For his work, Premier Kung-Sun was awarded with the lordship of fifteen cities. He was so admired and well honored that his nobility rivaled even that of Duke Shaw.

Less than a year later, the Duke fell ill and died. The prince who inherited the throne immediately dismissed Kung-Sun as the premier, because he hated him from the beginning. Then all of Kung-Sun's old enemies came out and induced the new Duke to issue a royal warrant for Kung-Sun's arrest. His title canceled and properties confiscated, Kung-Sun tried to flee to the neighboring Kingdom of Wei, but Wei hated him even more than Chin. He then escaped to a village in Chin, but a villager told him they dared not hide him because the law forbade it. Soon Kung-Sun was caught. At court accusations came from eight directions. Finally he was sentenced to a violent form of death.

Before his fall, several Taoist scholars whom he became acquainted with offered him two kinds of advice, because indeed he was a talented man.

> 1) After attaining great success, he should have guided Duke Shaw to change the style of management. He himself fully realized that the Legalist Style of Management alone could never last. It went against the principles of nature.

> 2) Retire after great success.

But Kung-Sun's greed and attitude prevented him from heeding good advice, thereby bringing about a sad end.

Because of his talents, the Kingdom of Chin was able to steadily build a strong foundation. Many years later it was to conquer six other kingdoms, unite China, and found the Chin Dynasty. Now every visitor to China will see the Great Wall and the Chin tomb in Hsian and leave remembering the accomplishments of the Chin

CONCLUSION

Dynasty, but how many of them know of Kung-Sun?

In Kung-Sun's story, you may find many valuable principles that may benefit your own practice. Throughout history he has served as a role model for management, good and bad points notwithstanding.

The moment the Kingdom of Chin conquered all of China, the moment the Dynasty began to crumble. The Dynasty barely survived through the next thirty-six years until it was replaced by the Han Dynasty, which practiced the teachings of the Yellow Emperor and Lao Tzu. When the management style was changed to the Integral Management of Tao, China entered her first golden age.

APPENDIX

EYE EXERCISES

People who suffer from eye problems usually suffer from nervous disorders, and vice-versa. As anger is a symptom of tension and fatigue, anger may be induced in those who use their eyes too much. The Internal Exercises for the eyes will strengthen both the eyes and the nervous system and help dissolve stress, tension, and fatigue.

Also, the eyes, specifically their movements, are indicative of an individual's intelligence. People who are clever have large eye movements and are always exploring their environment. Slow eye movement or a lack of eye movement indicates a repressed level of intelligence, which may also be helped through stimulation of the eyes.

Poor blood circulation, indicated by dark circles under the eyes, can also be helped by doing the Eye Exercises. Poor blood circulation results from long periods of physical inactivity, such as those spent behind a desk or meeting table. If circulation is sluggish, body temperature goes up. Then the blood "boils" and forms clots. High

APPENDIX

blood pressure and heart disease may occur. So in order to prevent blood clots, the Eye Exercises should be performed.

Doing the Eye Exercise can also help bags or puffiness under the eyes, which indicate water retention or bad metabolism. It also helps retard the signs of aging and improve youthful looks by exercising and toning the surrounding muscles and skin tissues.

1. Place thumbs on rim of the bony eye sockets at the upper inside corner of the eyes. There is a slight depression in the bone at the correct point. Those points are designated by the letter A in figure A.1a. Press in deeply. Any pain indicates some blockage. Then massage the points for a count of 10. Release. Repeat for a total of 3 times.

2. Next, place index fingers in the small depressions at the middle of the lower eye sockets—points designated by B. Press in deeply on the rims, not cheekbones. Massage for a count of 10. Release. Then repeat for a total of 3 times.

3. Then, place index fingers on lower eye socket $1/4$ of the distance from outside corners of the eyes. (Look for letter C in figure A.1a and d.) Press and massage for a count of 10. Release. Repeat for a total of 3 times.

4. Place thumbs on top of eye sockets about $1/3$ of the distance from the outside corners of the eyes. (Look for letter D.) Press and massage for a count of 10. Release. Repeat for a total of 3 times.

5. Place fingers on the temples by coming out from the end of the eyebrows and locating soft depressions on the sides of the head (point E). Press and massage for a count of 10. Release. Repeat for a total of 3 times.

6. Palming. Rub hands together briskly until they are quite warm. Cup the hands over both eyes, fingers slightly crossed,

APPENDIX

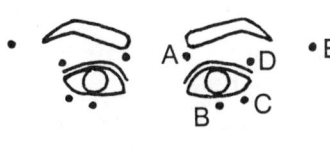
a.

b.

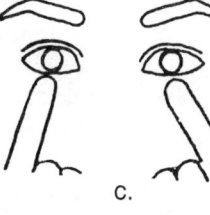
c.

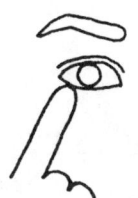

d.

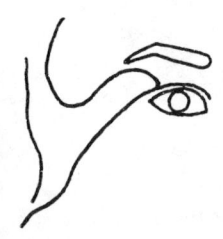
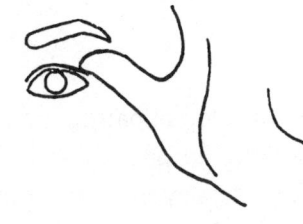
e.

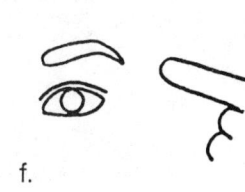
f.

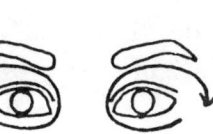
g.

Figure A.1a-g Eye Exercises

APPENDIX

right over left. Do not press the eyes. Hold for a count of 10. Then repeat for a total of 3 times, always feeling the warmth entering into the eyes from the hands.

7. Then rub eyes lightly with three middle fingers. Rub the bones around the eyes in a circular motion, starting from the inside corner of each eye next to the nose. Rub up the bridge of the nose, across the eyebrows, towards the temples, down and back around the lower rims of the eye sockets to the nose again. Do this 10 times. Pause. Repeat for a total of 3 cycles.

NOTE A: Rubbing in the opposite direction will weaken the eye muscles and cause wrinkles to appear.

NOTE B: For cataract or glaucoma, practice the first seven eye exercises up to 20 minutes daily. Whenever your eyes are tired, do the Eye Exercises, as they will completely revitalize your entire body in minutes. It is also good to do them in conjunction with exercises which strengthen the liver. (For background details please refer to *The Complete System of Self-Healing*.)

NOTE C: Once you have located the painful points, it is not necessary to continue pressing hard on these points. When you are doing the Eye Exercises, even a very light touching of the points will accomplish the purpose of the exercise, which is to restore normal vision.

NOTE D: Use the first two points (A and B) for diagnosis. If it is painful at all when you press in deeply, then there is something wrong with the eyes and/or body. If it is puffy or dark under point B, water retention or lack of proper rest is indicated.

One may also practice additional exercises which will strengthen the eyes and the muscles surrounding them.

APPENDIX

1. Begin by keeping the head straight, but with the eyes first looking up toward the ceiling and then down at the floor. Repeat this motion several times. The eyes should always move slowly and with deliberation.

2. Next, look to either side of the head.

3. Then look up and down into the opposite corners of the eyes.

4. Then rotate the eyes first in a clockwise direction, then in a counterclockwise direction. This will take about ten minutes to perform when done slowly.

5. Always follow these eye movements with a rubbing of the hands and a pressing of the palms onto the eyes to bring heat and energy into them.

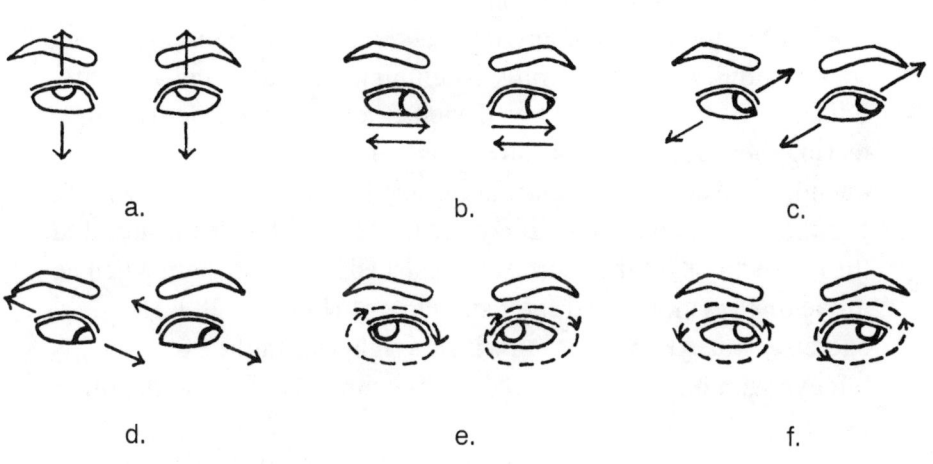

Figure A.2a-f Eye Motions

If you practice these exercises consistently over a period of time, you may never need glasses to see clearly.

The following is an example of how the exercise is utilized. A student of mine and his family benefited greatly from the Eye Exercises. His problems first began after he left his job in the computer department of a San Francisco telephone company for a better job in San Jose. Because he was working as a trainee on three months probation at the San Jose company, his wife—then working as a nurse in a San Francisco hospital—could not leave her job and move away from San Francisco. Plus their house and four children were in San Francisco. So even if he was tired after hours of heavy concentration and computer training, he still had to drive for a total of 3 hours to and from work and fight traffic.

When he got home, he was usually overwhelmed by the demands of his four children. Not being able to stand the noise any longer, he usually retreated to his bedroom, locked the door, and collapsed on the bed. It was not long before his miserable outlook on life, lack of appetite for his wife's cooking, and indifference toward family and marital matters started explosive fights between him and his equally strained wife. Soon they agreed to a divorce.

But before they took any legal action, they came to my office seeking advice. After carefully listening to both husband and wife, I discovered that they still loved each other and that the only things tearing them apart were the stress and tension of overwork. Consequently, I asked them to delay taking any legal action for two weeks, enough time to let the Eye Exercises take effect. I gave the husband the instructions for the exercises and asked him to do them when he drove on the emptier and safer stretches of Highway 280. He could exercise both eyes by steering with the right hand as he exercised his left eye with his left hand and then switching hands to do the other eye.

A month or so later they both came back to my office bearing a gift. The husband said the Eye Exercises performed a miracle on their lives. When he exercised his eyes as he drove, he was never tired when he reached home—he felt completely refreshed. He was able to play with his children, answer their questions, even help them

Appendix

do their homework; his appetite returned; he was able to fulfill his marital duties; and he was able to concentrate on his job and pass probation smoothly. Afterwards, he was formally hired, and he was able to sell the house in San Francisco and move to San Jose. His wife also found a new job in San Jose, and their children were happy. They said they were starting a new life with more love for each other than ever before.

STOMACH RUBBING EXERCISE

When it comes to stress management there is another exercise, the Stomach Rubbing Exercise, for reducing stress and tension immediately. The exercise is also excellent for removing excess weight and reducing high blood pressure, while producing many other benefits. It is easy to do and completely safe, and it could be done anywhere, anytime. No equipment is necessary.

1. Begin by lying down flat on your back. Relax.

2. Put the palm of your hand on your navel. (If you are right handed, use your right hand; if left handed, use your left hand.) Then start to rub clockwise from the center—that is, from the right to the left—first in small circles and then gradually expand the movement until the upper and lower limits of the stomach and abdomen are being rubbed (see figure A.3a-b).

3. When you have completed the first movement, then reverse it, rubbing counterclockwise in smaller and smaller circles until you are back to the center of the navel. You need not press down with any force. Apply a slight pressure as you rub slowly.

APPENDIX

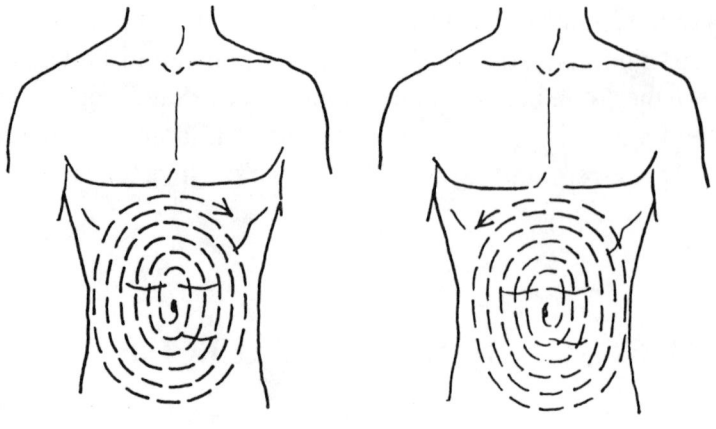

a. Clockwise Rubbing   b. Counterclockwise Rubbing

Figure A.3a-b

4. Repeat this clockwise and counterclockwise motion as many times as you wish.

NOTE A: When you do the exercise, concentrate on feeling the heat (energy) from your hands penetrate into the stomach tissues. Do not let your mind wander; the mental actions must coincide with the physical actions, to bring maximum effectiveness. If concentration is broken, the exercise must be started again from the beginning.

NOTE B: A brisker version of the Stomach Rubbing Exercise also exists. You may begin this exercise by rubbing the palms of the hands together vigorously and placing the hands, palms down, on the lower abdomen so that they lie on either side of the navel. Now begin to rub both sides of the abdomen briskly, following the pattern depicted in figure

APPENDIX

A.4. Rub so that both hands meet near the navel on the downswing. Keep on rubbing until the friction heats up the abdominal tissues. You may repeat this exercise as many times as you wish. This version of the exercise brings more stimulation and energy to the abdomen than the regular version, so it can be used for debilitating diseases of the internal organs and peristaltic problems. It is especially good for trimming down the girth.

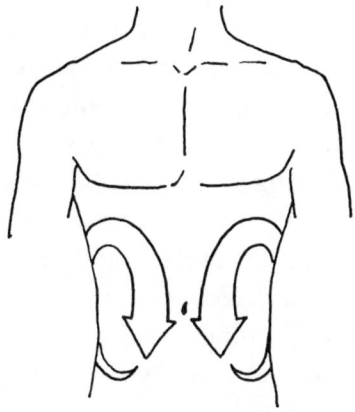

Figure A.4 Stomach Rubbing (Brisker Version)

Fatty accumulations and deposits are disturbed from their resting place and eventually broken up. They are then passed into the eliminatory system and out of the body. By such apparently simple means, the superfluous areas of the stomach and abdomen are literally rubbed away.

When you rub in a clockwise direction—which again, is from your right to your left in gradually widening circles—you are encouraging proper and easeful bowel movement. Quite often constipation is a symptom indicating that the large intestine is overfunctioning. The large intestine is absorbing too much water from the waste matter as it passes through on its way to the rectum.

APPENDIX

This causes the waste matter to be compacted to the point where the normal peristaltic activity of the large intestine is not sufficient to expel the waste matter. Constipation results and fecal material that would normally have been passed on through the anus are stored in the body. The clockwise motion augments the peristaltic activity and slows down the water removal process to normal levels.

One young woman I taught this exercise to told me she had suffered from constipation most of her life. She was only 23 years old, but she had been suffering from constipation for 15 years. She had tried drugs, laxatives, and enemas. But nothing she did eliminated the problem. And yet, from the first week she began doing this exercise, she ceased to have problems with bowel movements. She felt, by her own admission, like a new person. She told me later that after three months of doing the exercise, her whole digestive system evened out and she never had the same problem again.

Rubbing in a counterclockwise motion has the opposite effect—that of helping to solidify fecal material as it passes through the intestine. It does this by stimulating the passage of water from the large intestine to the kidneys. An extreme case of chronic diarrhea which was corrected with this simple technique was recently brought to my attention. One of my students told me that ten years ago his mother had been operated on for cancer of the colon. Since that time, she has had absolutely no control over her bowel movements. She could not even go out for fear she would suddenly find she had to use the bathroom and not have access to one. Her son taught her the stomach rubbing technique. She had tried every other remedy by that time and was ready for anything that held some promise of helping her. After a few days of practicing the exercise, her stools formed for the first time in ten years. Since then she has been able to normalize her life, and the problem has ceased to plague her.

Rubbing the abdomen in both the clockwise and counterclockwise directions will help stomach ulcers. One case demonstrating the exercise's efficaciousness is that of a 96-year-old Chinese senator. He tackles his duties with more enthusiasm and energy than people one-fourth his age. He is also actively involved in many different activities. Yet, he is never sick. His blood pressure, checked every morning by a government-appointed nurse, is always normal. When admirers ask him about his secret of youth, he tells them a story about a youthful experience. As a young man, he suffered from painful stomach ulcers, tuberculosis, and other diseases. When he served in the army, he sought medical help from doctors wherever he was stationed. Then one day, someone told him about a famous, aged healer who lived deep in the mountains. So he made an appointment to see the healer and struggled over the rocky terrain to see him. Having reached his destination, the young man greeted the healer and began a monologue about himself and his problems. But the old man continued to meditate and seemed to ignore the visitor; he did not open his eyes or speak. Finally, the healer uttered, "Go home and rub your stomach." Further questioning drew no replies. Disappointed at the simple remark, the young man struggled home. Back home, disappointment, exhaustion, and anger caused the ulcer to flare up again. Left with no alternative, the young man reluctantly rubbed his stomach. Immediately the pain faded away. Encouraged, he began to rub his stomach faithfully. A few months later, the ulcer completely disappeared. Gradually the tuberculosis disappeared also. His health improved daily. Seventy years later he still rubs his stomach daily, after every meal and whenever he feels uncomfortable.

The first year I was invited to lecture at the University of Oslo in Norway, one of the subjects I dwelt on was the Stomach Rubbing Exercise. The following year, I was invited back to lecture before an overcrowded audience again. Before I started speaking, an old man in the audience interrupted me and requested permission to speak. He told the audience to listen to me because whatever I said would be beneficial. Then he told everybody a story. He said that he attended my first lecture with a distended abdomen full of water

APPENDIX

because he was suffering from terminal liver cancer. He was in terrible pain. The doctors gave him only a few weeks to live. Every week he had to go to the hospital to have his abdomen pumped to remove the water. Desperate to try anything, he attended the lecture. That night, after learning about the stomach rubbing technique, he went home and rubbed his stomach. The pain went away and water never collected in his stomach again. One week later, he went to see his doctor and astonished him. His doctor exclaimed, "This is a miracle! I can't believe it! What did you do?" He replied, "I didn't do anything. I just rubbed my stomach." Thereafter, he faithfully rubbed his stomach. His liver did not bother him anymore, though it was still cancerous. He was able to discontinue chemotherapy. Furthermore, he had become "healthy," and he was able to go back to work. When I returned to Norway the third year, the man was still around.

The efficaciousness of the exercise is explained by the penetration of energy from the hand into the abdominal tissues. Energy penetration can be augmented by making use of your sensory powers. Feel the energy from your hand penetrate into the skin and organs underneath. You should also feel that the energy is being retained and that it is heating up your abdominal tissues. As more energy penetrates your body, the area around your navel will begin to burn as if a fire had been started within. Achieving this sensation requires a great deal of concentration and patience, and it should be done every time you do the exercise. (For further details, please refer to *The CompleteSystem of Self-Healing*.)

TAO OF BALANCED DIET

The following is an excerpt from the June 1, 1988 issue of the New York Times. (For further details, please refer to *The Tao of*

Appendix

Balanced Diet: Secrets of a Thin and Healthy Body.)

For most people, food serves many purposes: it fuels the body, pleases the palate and satisfies the soul. But increasingly, Americans are also looking to food to prevent disease and promote good health. They cut out egg yolks to avoid cholesterol, load up on fresh vegetables and high-fiber cereals to reduce cancer risks and drink low-fat milk to stave off osteoporosis.

One nontraditional system that seems to be growing in popularity is the ancient Chinese philosophy of Taoism, which explains the world in terms of opposites and seeks to find ways to keep conflicting forces in balance. It advocates a system of eating as well as the use of herbs to maintain health.

There are more people now than five years ago offering advice on how to heal with foods and herbs, using Chinese concepts. One of them is John Lindseth, who founded the Tao Healing Arts Society in New York. Like many Americans who practice nontraditional methods of healing, Mr. Lindseth learned about Taoism through personal need. Fifteen years ago, when he was working as a psychotherapist in San Francisco, he developed Guillain-Barre syndrome, a debilitating neurological disorder.

When doctors said they could do nothing for him, Mr. Lindseth went to see Dr. Chang, the author, who gave him dietary advice and herbal formulations. The success of the treatment prompted Mr. Lindseth to study Taoism further.

Taoists use the properties of food and of herbs to restore balance to an ailing body. They divide food into five categories, based on taste. Each category is thought to nourish a certain organ of the body as well as the physical functions and emotional states that relate to that organ: bitter foods affect the heart and small intestine; salty foods, the kidney and bladder; sweet foods, the spleen-pancreas and stomach; sour foods, the liver and gallbladder; and spicy foods, the lungs and large intestine.

Ideally, Taoists believe, a diet should include equal parts of each type of food. If there is too much or too little of one category, the related organ will be adversely affected. Thus, if someone eats too much salty food, the kidneys will be stressed; if another eats too little bitter food, the heart will be weakened.

Taoists say that many Americans eat too many sweet and salty foods, a fact also bemoaned by traditionally trained nutritionists. Shellie Goldstein, a New Yorker who studied with Mr. Lindseth after getting a master's degree in nutrition from the University of Bridgeport, said that most people she sees have a highly restricted and monotonous diet, eating just 20 or 25 foods.

She advises clients to vary their diets and to increase their intake of herbs. As with many who resort to nontraditional approaches to matters of health, some clients are satisfied if their symptoms are relieved and do not care about the theories.

"I didn't get into that part of it," said Nancy Trent, the owner of a New York public-relations company who consulted Ms. Goldstein because she felt continually tired. "If it works, don't ask. Just do it."

MORNING AND EVENING PRAYERS

They are the best remedies for marital discord, unlike divorce. Generally marital discord begins in bed and concludes in court. The bed reveals many imperfections in both men and women, whether the imperfections are the inability to care for others, sexual inability, etc. Because people are imperfect, they have many lessons to learn and many shortcomings to correct. If people are unable to face their lessons and shortcomings and learn and correct them, the resulting discord causes anger, frustration, estrangement, broken homes, psychological disorders, plummeting productiveness in the work place, and societal incapableness.

APPENDIX

Man and woman should live together—not necessarily in the sense of physical cohabitation, but in the sense of mental and spiritual coexistence, made possible by a sexual relationship. Men and women need each other for satisfying, for healing, balancing, and adjusting their physical bodies. For such purposes, the Morning and Evening Prayers are strongly recommended.

To perform the Morning Prayer, man and woman should assume the missionary position. Then, with eyes closed, they should lock themselves together with their mouths, legs, and arms. The man should penetrate and use just enough movement to maintain an erection. (He should not ejaculate.) Then the couple enjoys and shares the feelings derived from such closeness and stillness for as long as they desire. Just as you start the day with Morning Prayer, conclude the day with Evening Prayer, which is performed like the Morning Prayer. The Morning Prayer enlivens the body, and the Evening Prayer relaxes the body.

During the Prayers, the couple rise beyond space and time, even if the Prayers last for only two minutes, which is in itself an infinity. Man and woman become locked together in a meeting of minds. The nature of the attraction becomes mental. Following the Morning or Evening Prayer, the woman becomes completely open and receptive, completely Yin. After the Morning or Evening Prayer, the man is completely giving, completely Yang. Her complete Yin state and his complete Yang state constitute a perfect Yin-Yang balance. This balance generates a cycle of harmony, creativity, and love.

The following is an example of the Prayers' utilization. After having counseled many people who face divorce or family discord, I found that Prayers solved problems quickly and effectively. Before the Prayers are utilized, a typical example of family life is as follows.

A lifeless husband comes home after a hard day at work. His lonely wife tries to make conversation with him by talking about trivialities. The husband cannot bear listening to these things, but he grits his teeth, and, with the greatest of patience and tolerance, makes it through the evening. But his actions are cold. His wife notices his attitude and begins to think that he does not love her anymore.

Then, once in bed, to show his wife his love, he makes love to her. But in his tired and stressed condition, he could only bring her to a partial orgasm, before he rolls over and snores. She, however, lies awake unable to reach heaven or earth. She tosses back and forth, full of anger and frustration. She may even have to clean up the mess her husband made. Finally sleep envelops her at dawn.

Just then, the husband wakes up, wakes his wife, and demands, "Honey, where's the coffee?" The wife, head aching and tired, snaps, "Make it yourself!"

The husband, silenced, leaves the house hungry and angry, fights traffic, and begins a day at the office in bad humor. He unloads his anger on his co-workers. Then they get mad and make work difficult for him. Performance and efficiency plummets. Only the greatest tolerance and patience helps him survive through the day. Meanwhile, all morning, the wife tries to dispel her headache with Tylenol. Her headache finally disappears before her husband gets home, but her loneliness and dissatisfaction have grown greater.

When her husband does come home after fighting traffic, she tries to talk to him, to dispel the loneliness and dissatisfaction. Instead, she carries on a monologue, which he drowns out with television, radio, etc. She is deeply hurt by this. Tension fills the air. There is a limit to everyone's endurance. Then, over a matter of the tiniest importance, both explode. They try to make up but they go to bed and make the same mistakes again.

Day after day of the same things finally drive them to divorce. The family will be broken, jobs will be lost, and a part of society will collapse.

Such things need not and do not happen when the Prayers are performed. Many couples on the brink of divorce have experienced a complete change in attitude and life. Husbands and wives never have enough of each other. They sleep restfully after the Evening

APPENDIX

Prayer. After the Morning Prayer, wives usually hop out of bed to prepare an excellent breakfast and send their husbands off to the office with kisses. The husbands usually arrive at the office thinking the world is wonderful. They treat everyone well, and their kindness is usually returned. Office affairs become smoother and less stressful. At the end of the day, husbands usually cannot wait to go home to tell their wives about their successes and talk and listen to them. Traffic does not bother them. When they do get home, a wonderful dinner is ready. This pattern of life saves the marriage, the family, the company, the society, and eventually the entire nation.

The purpose of the Morning and Evening Prayers is to turn the bond between husband and wife into a bond of True, or Divine, Love. True Love cannot be taught; it does not come from the mind like romantic love. True Love has spiritual origins, as it is released from the heart during the Morning and Evening Prayers. Unlike romantic love, True Love is giving. During the Morning or Evening Prayers, man and woman melt together, laying aside their egos to exchange energies to heal each other. Once released, this love will permeate their everyday lives. Their love, rippling through society, will affect society positively.

INDEX

A

Achievement, 62, 64
Accounting, 110, 112, 236
Adam, sons of, 118
Advertising, 236
Age,
    of Celestial Immortal, 44-45
    of Evil Men, 42-43
    of Gentlemen, 44
    of Littlemen, 43-44
    of Terrestrial Immortal, 44
    of Transformed Immortal, 44
Ambition, 62
Analysis, 168-177
    determination of benefits, 171-177
    Five-Star Relations, 168-170, 171
Anger, 191, 245
    dissipation of, 245-251, 258-261
    use of, 191-192
Arrogance, 64
Art of War, 58, 145
Attitudes, Eight, 64-78, 235, 236
    Japanese adaptation of, 76-77
    of Earth (stopping, etc.), 73-74
    of Fire (giving, mutual benefit, etc.), 72-73
    of Heaven (constant improvement, goals, etc.), 65-66
    of Lake (uplifting recreation, etc.), 75-76
    of Mountain (tolerance, etc.), 68-69
    of Thunder (creativity, etc.), 70
    of Water (discipline, etc.), 67-69
    of Wind (penetration, will, etc.), 71-72

B

Balanced Diet, 236, 256-258
Board of Directors, 236
Bodily organs and bowels, 79-98, 245-246
    affects on decision making, 159-160, 180, 185, 245-246
    exercises for, 79-84, 245-254
Blessings, Eight, 78
Brain, 93-94, 98, 159
    affects on decision making, 159
    affects on personality, 93-94
    divisions of, 93-98
    trust, 183-184
Buddhist monk, 193-195
Budget, 147-148, 236

C

Carlson, Ed, 166

INDEX

Centrifugal Perception, 120-122
Centripetal Perception, 121-122
CEO, 59, 236
Chairman of the Board, 116, 236
Chang, Commander, 129-132, 139-140, 142-143, 146, 148, 149
Chang, Liang, 133-135
Charisma, gaining, 203
Chen, Ping, 47
Chiang, Shang, 17-21, 45, 90, 135
Chin Dynasty, 133, 243-244
Chin Shih Huang, Emperor, 54, 133
Chou Dynasty, 21, 22, 64, 237
Chuan Tzu, 148, 225
Chu-Ko, Liang, 184
Circle, Psycho-Dynamics of, 124
Classics of the Internal, 48, 94
Classic of Purity, 52
Communication,
    skill of, 141
    Style of, 25-26, 29, 59
    techniques of, 205-223
Competitiveness, 70, 77, 78
Component Line, Psycho-Dynamics of, 123
Composition, 177-179
Concentration, 71
Conduct, for greater effectiveness, 220-221
Conference, 236
Confucius, 2, 65
Constipation, 253
Controller, 110, 112, 114-115, 236
    role of, 114-115
Co-worker, 87, 88, 170
Corporate structure, 114, 235, 236

Creativity, 70
Cycle of Degeneration, 49-50, 95-96, 111, 112
Cycle of Generation, 49-50, 95-96, 111, 112

D

Decision making, 138-140, 160
    brain trust, 183-184
    guidelines for, 160-162
    health affecting, 180
    information for, 163-166
    Japanese, 180-183
    results, 184-185
    styles, 180-184
    wrong, 179-180
Deeds, 41
Diarrhea, 254
Diplomacy, Style of, 27, 29
Directionology for mental attitudes, 78-84
Discipline, 67-68
Dynasty,
    Chin, 133, 243-244
    Chou, 21, 22, 64, 237
    Fu Hsi, 64
    Han, 47, 114, 134, 168, 244
    T'ang, 47, 115

E

Earth,
    Attitude of, 73-74
    Personality, 98, 107-109
Education, 77, 236
Ego, 61-62, 219
Egotism, 219-220
    minimizing, 219

of subordinates, 219-220
of superior, 219-220
Eight Attitudes, see Attitudes
Ellipse, Psycho-Dynamics of, 129
Emotion, 38, 39, 159
Emperor, role of, 114-116
Evolution, 33, 42, 45, 55, 75-76
   mission, 45, 55, 62
   retrogression, 41, 76
Eve, sons of, 118
Evil Men, 36, 38, 42-43
   Age of 42-43
Eye Exercises, 245-251

F
Fear, 190
Finance, 236
Fire,
   Attitude of, 72-73
   Personality, see below
Five-Element Personality, 98-109, 159
   combinative effects of, 101, 103, 105, 107, 109
   effects of co-workers, 111
   Earth, 98, 107-109
   Fire, 98, 103-105, 111
   Metal, 98, 101-103
   Water, 98, 99-101, 111
   Wood, 98, 105-107, 111
Five-Element Theory, 95-98, 111, 168, 171, 175
Five-Star System, 95, 99-103, 177, 207, 226
   matching to jobs, 110
   matching to personalities, 111
   organization, 112-114

Five Yin-Yang Personalities, see also Five-Element Personality, 94-95, 98, 109
Fu Hsi Dynasty, 64

G
Gentlemen, 36-37, 42, 44, 65
   Age of, 44
Giving, 72-73
Goals, 65-67
God, 38-39, 48, 49, 56, 66, 91, 126, 189, 195
Government,
   Five-Element Functions of, 112, 115
   structure of, 48, 114-116
   types of, 42
   U.S., 113
Greater Yang Personality, 94, 98, 109
Greater Yin Personality, 94, 98, 109
Greed, 137, 153, 227-231
Growth, 225-226

H
Han Dynasty, 47, 114, 134, 168, 244
   government structure of, 114
   principles of government, 47
Hatoyama, Takuya, 157
Health-care, 184, 236
Heart, 79-98
   affect on thought, 159
   exercises for, 82
Heaven, Attitude of, 65-66, 236
Hexagram, *"Sun,"* 125-126

INDEX

Hsiang-Pi, 211
Hsien (immortal), 36
Human beings, 36-37, 227
    Evil Men, 36, 38, 42, 43
    Gentlemen, 36, 37, 42, 44, 65
    Littlemen, 36, 42, 43, 44
Human nature, 117-119, 122-126
    five weaknesses of, 190-191
Hyperbola, Psycho-Dynamics of, 125

I
I-Ching, 195
Illness, 190
Immortal, 17, 36-42, 189
Information, 163-166, 236
Internal Exercises, 78, 159, 185, 236
    Eye Exercise, 245-251
    East, 81-82
    North, 78
    Northeast, 81
    Northwest, 79
    South, 83
    Southeast, 82
    Southwest, 83
    West, 84
Intercommunication, 187-223
    Intercourse Chaos, 189
    Internal Message Chaos, 188-189
    interpretation, see below
    persuasion of leaders, 203- 223
    persuasion of subordinates, 200-223
Interpretation, 193-199
    Essence of Movement, 196
    evidence for, 197
    picturing, 196
    unmistaken conclusion, 197
Instincts, 38, 40, 43, 187
Invention, 112, 236

J
Japanese,
    adaptation of Eight Attitudes, 76-77
    adaptation of Subtle Casket, 235
    management of, 66
    mentor-protege system of, 77-78
    decision making of, 180-183
    teamwork of, 78
    training of managers, 77
    working spirit of, 182
Jesus, 191-192, 214, 215, 216
    Eight Blessings of, 78
Job, 49
Joy, 191

K
Kidney, 79-98
    affect on decision making, 169
    exercise for, 80
Kingdom,
    of Animals, 33, 34
    of God, 33, 35, 36, 228, 229
    of Humankind 33, 35, 36, 57
    of Mineral, 33-34
    of Vegetation, 33-34
Kuei Ku Tzu, 58, 59, 66, 69, 85, 57, 88, 163, 189, 195, 196, 205, 206, 207, 208, 209, 210, 211,

212

Kuei Ku Tzu, 58, 178, 205
Kung-Sun, Yang, 237-244

L

Lake, Attitude of, 75-76
Lao Tzu, 3, 27, 28, 40, 42, 52, 53, 54, 56, 57, 67, 69, 72, 74, 76, 89, 113, 115, 122, 135, 144, 155, 185, 186, 187, 189, 191, 203, 222, 229, 230, 244
Law,
    of Cyclicalness (Cause and Effect), 27, 52-53, 62
    of Growth, 53-54
    of Imperfection, 57
    of Loss and Gain, 54-55
    of Time, 55
    of Utility, 56-57
Leadership, 55-56, 89, 129, 133, 236
    of Fear, 156
    of Happiness, 156
    of Hate, 155
    impression on followers, 138
    insecurities of, 152
    of Invisibility, 156
    nine rules of, 45, 46
    organization of, 148-150
    quality of, 135-136
    persuasion of subordinates, 199-223
    power of 140-148
    responsibilities of, 136-137
    sacrifices of, 150-152
Lee, Chung-Wu, 118-119, 120, 153
Legalist, Style of, 23-24, 29, 239,

243
Lesser Yang Personality, 94, 98, 109
Lesser Yin Personaltiy, 94, 98, 109
Lincoln, Abraham, 66, 74
Littlemen, 36, 42, 43, 44
    Age of 44
Liver, 79-98
    cancer of, 256
    affect on thinking process, 159-160
    exercise for, 82
Loyalty, 22, 23, 45, 71
Lungs, 79-98
    affect on emotion, 159
    exercise for, 83

M

Magnetic Field, 119-121, 176
Management, 45, 117
    Japanese, see also Japanese, 66
    styles of, 22-29, 235
Manager, 21, 77, 93, 110, 225
Marketing, 236
Matsushita Electric Co., 66, 77
Matsushita, Konosuke, 66, 161, 166, 183
Mencius, 89, 117, 118, 226, 231
Mental body, 34, 35, 38-40, 188, 227
Mentor-Protege system, 77-78, 85
Mercifulness, 71
Messages, 187-193
Metal Personality, 98, 101-103
Militarism, Style of, 26-27, 145, 165

INDEX

Mission, 55-56, 62, 223
Mo, Style of, 24
Money, rules of, 228-229
Moses, 90-91
Motivation, see also Intercommunication and Leadership, 46, 86
Mountain, Attitude of, 68-69, 236

N
Negotiation, 27, 236
New employees, 236

O
Ocean, spirit of, 67
Open-mindedness, 135
Over-reaction, 145

P
Pa-Kua, 1, 235
Pao Pu Tzu, 41
Parabola, Psycho-Dynamics of, 124
Parallel Line, Psycho-Dynamics of, 123
People, dealing with right, 93
Person, becoming right, 61, 77-78, 93
Personality, see also Five Yin-Yang Personalities, 94-95, 109
Persuasion, 26, 141, 199-223
    classification of people, 207-209
    confidence, 205-206
    Forbiddens, 203
    impression, 203-205
    ordinary, 203-223
    presentation, 214-218
    Principles of Advantage and Disadvantage, 209-214
    reflex, 206-207
    rule of orders, 201
    skills, 212
    suggestion, 218-223
Physical body, 34-35, 38-40, 189, 227
Plain Book, 133-134
Planning, 65-66, 236
Position, 87
    preservation of, 86, 155
    right, 85, 93
President, 116
Prime minister, 47, 57, 114-116
Principles of Advantage and Disadvantage, 209-214
Productivity, 25, 236, 254, 261
Promotion, 87, 88
Psycho-Dynamics, 119-126, 210
    Centrifugal Perception, 120-122
    Centripetal Perception, 121-122
    principle of loss, 125-126
Punishment, 23-24, 62

Q
Quality control, 236
Quaternary Logic, 178, 215-218

R
Recreation, 75-76
Reflex, 206-207
Research, 110, 236

INDEX

Resultant Line, Psycho-Dynamics of, 123
Retribution, 52, 155
Reward, 23, 62, 86, 144

S

Sacrifice, of leader, 67
Sages, 66, 76, 88, 222
Satan, 48-49
Scheme, 26-27
   of Jurisdiction, 153
   of Pretense, 153
   Swindling, 154
Scholar, Style of, 22-23, 29
Sex,
   affect on work performance, 258-261
   improvement of, 254
Shaw, Duke, 238-241, 243
Shimomura, Kiyoshi, 223
Solomon, King, 56, 71, 190, 227
Spiritual body, 34-35, 38-40, 188, 227
Straight Line, Psycho-Dynamics of, 123
Straight talk, 197
Stress, reduction of, 245, 251-256, 258-261
Strength, 22, 69
Su, Chin, 58-59
Su Shu, 133-134
Subordinates, 117, 219-220
Subtle Casket, 234
   blueprint of, 236
Sun, Pin, 58, 146
Sun Tzu, 26, 27, 145, 164, 165
Superior, 86, 218-222

Supposition, 167-168
Suspicion, 167

T

Takeda, Yutaka, 223
T'ang Dynasty, 47, 115
   government structure of, 115
   principles of government, 47
Tao, 38, 40, 42, 44, 57, 222
Tao, Style of, 28
Tao of Sexology, 236
Taoism, 37, 41, 42, 56, 62, 95, 96, 189, 229
Taoist scholars, 35, 36, 48, 50, 54, 56, 66, 93, 98, 162, 184, 215, 243
Teamwork, 78-79, 111-112
Tension, reduction of, 245-251, 258
Theory X and Y, 117
Thought, 38-39, 160
Thought process, 26, 167-179
Time, 55-56, 89
Thunder, Attitude of, 70
Tolerance, 69
Tokugawa, Iyeyasu, 77
Trigrams, 62-64
   Earth, 62, 73
   East, 62
   Fire, 62, 72
   Heaven, 62, 65
   Lake, 62, 75-76
   Mountain, 62, 68
   North, 62
   Northeast, 62
   Northwest, 62
   South, 62
   Southeast, 62

INDEX

Southwest, 62
Thunder, 62, 70
Water, 62, 67
West, 62
Wind, 62, 71

U
Ulcer, 255
United Airlines, 166

W
Washington, George, 56, 74
Water,
    Attitude of, 67-69
    Personality, 98, 99-101, 111
    wisdom of, 28-29
Wealth, 22, 69, 228-229
Weight reduction, 251-256
Wen, Emperor, 47
Wen, King, 64
Will, 38-39, 71
Wind, Attitude of, 71-72
Wood Personality, 98, 105-107, 111
Working Spirit, 146
Worry, 190
Wu, King, 21, 45, 238
Wu-pu-wei, 89, 115, 135
Wu-wei, 89, 115, 135

Y
Yang lines, 62, 65, 67, 68, 69, 70, 71, 72, 75
Yang Tzu, 191
Yao, Emperor, 156-157, 238
Yellow Emperor, 2, 48, 94, 101, 109, 114, 144, 145, 244
Yellow Stone Sage, 133-135, 141, 147, 148, 152, 153, 166, 176, 185, 188, 191, 203, 218, 221
Yen, Yin, 223
Yin lines, 62, 67, 68, 69, 70, 71, 72, 73, 75
Yin-Yang, 48-58, 62, 93, 125, 172, 205
    Cycles of, 111, 112
    interaction of, 49-52
    laws of, 52-58
    Style of, 27-29
Yin-Yang Balanced Personality, 94, 98, 109
Yu-wei, 89, 115, 135

• •

Within a year of publication, we received a great many letters, all extremely meaningful. Here, a few important ones have been specially selected for your reference.

"The vast scope of the lessons, illustrations and manner of presenting the essential prerequisites for successfully handling the problems of today, while simply presented in this book, are so complete that if the reader were to digest and put into practice the centuries of wisdom contained within its covers the results would be tremendously rewarding.

"You offer a veritable foolproof blueprint for successful and healthy existence in a world beset with fear and unhappiness. The reader who intelligently studies your words of wisdom will find himself the recipient of success and happiness which comes to those who are willing to heed the teachings from higher spheres.

"Among my almost a thousand volumes I treasure yours most highly and it occupies a 'must' in my library as it should for others.

"My appreciation to you for this priceless gift to humanity extends beyond a simple 'Thanks' because the rewards which I and other readers can anticipate and receive from our intelligent use of this knowledge can extend far beyond our highest expectations."

—**Leonard A. Worthington, J.D., LL.D.; Director Emeritus, Hastings College of Law, University of California**

"THE BOOK IS WONDERFUL AND THANKS A MILLION. It did make me feel inferior in as much as what I discovered at SRI seems to have been known some 4,000 years ago. I was humbled by this book and loved it. . . .

"As you know I was part of a research team in 'management science' set up by Stanford Research Institute from 1965 through 1970. Our research resulted in statistically discovering the 3 factors which statistically (Chi Square test for significants set at 0.997) separates successful companies and people from mediocrity are:

1) Continued Education of <u>senior</u> people
2) Overt Attention to resourcing the organisation or person (purchasing) and
3) Written down short term plans for improvement

"I was disappointed to discover that these factors were already known in 1,200 BC and that Dr. Chang has written on this in Chapter V. The Kingdom of God.

"Equally interesting is the comparison of Tao to Dr. Otis Benepe who created in our research the Matrix which set out what actions would survive and what actions would die. . . . This same knowledge existing before our time embarrassed me a bit in that we didn't read Sage Kuei Ku's book and *Su Shu* Yellow Stone Sage's *Plain Book* earlier. It could have helped our work.

"The justification of the need for management as explained on page 45 should be read by everyone, as well as the last paragraph on page 46.

"The comment of the 'importance of retribution' page 53 is significant and bears reading as well as the 'faster growth brings earlier death.' In our studies of product life cycles those products which are developed quickly die quickly ie toys, fashion, many convenience foods, and services shows that not much has changed since 1,200 BC.

"Page 54 which covers the need of a good leader—to make educational, training and motivational policies that do not elevate expectations excessively; when plans are made, take care to consider potential problems as well as benefits. These principles we found are necessary in business and management planning work both in the USA and Britain.

"'Wise men know how to divide their shares' is a principle which should be practiced widely. Regretfully because this is not practiced, this has been the root of much unrest and bankruptcies in this country since 1974 when Opec really disturbed our world.

"We have found that Dr. Chang is right when he writes 'when Gigantic egos are coupled with gigantic ambitions, they cause endless frustration and depression, mental illness, and crime.'

"'And that managers should submit three plans every year; six month plans, two year plans, five year plans and monthly revisions of these plans' is a principle which we find leads to success; less than this leads to mediocrity.

"I can go on and on about Dr. Chang's book and the importance of these concepts and ideas to managers who today want to cope with the complexities of their working life."

  —Albert S. Humphrey, Chairman, Business Planning and Development, London

"After attending business school and reading numerous books and articles about management practices, this book has given me a fresh look at handling tough management issues. I have to agree that the Taoist's method described in this book is indeed very simple, easy and effective.

"Considering that the Japanese are doing so well in their management practices by using only part of the knowledge mentioned in this book, we can certainly benefit a lot and drastically increase our productivity by learning and implementing the management style of Tao.

"Thank you for another masterpiece after your several books published previously. I certainly would recommend this book to anyone interested in the area of management."

—Tony W. Lin, Harvard MBA; Vice President/Chief Financial Officer, Therma Wave, Inc.

"Thank you for writing *The Integral Management of Tao*. This book has changed my life visibly in just a few short months that I have been studying it. A few more prominent ways include:

"Since reorganizing our business according to the principles of the Five Star System, our . . .

- Sales have more than doubled.
- We have been able to select and hire the appropriately qualified people to balance our corporate team resulting in greatly improved work efficiency and harmony of working relations.
- The direction of our growth is more clearly defined as our creativity is considerably sharper.
- There is an increased sense or feeling of security that the newly organized and more balanced corporate structure gives.
- Our marketing efforts have become very sharp and focused, resulting in our associating with brokers in 27 states.
- As a result of the Eight Attitudes, my work is more focused, more disciplined, and my interaction with my associates is very smooth.
- In communications, the most immediately useful tool has been information on how to speak to people according to their background. This has been invaluable in allowing me to adjust my communications to give the appropriate response. This has resulted in retaining a higher percentage of clients with a correspondingly improved income.

"The examples could, without doubt, go on and on. This is the single most practical and useful book for daily living and working that I've seen. I have studied these subjects for years, ranging from taking all of the Dale Carnegie courses to being trained in psychology. Compared to *The Integral Management of Tao*, these sources pale."
  —**John Lindseth, President, Long Life Products, Inc.**

"I wanted to write to you to let you know how useful the information in *The Integral Management of Tao* has been.

"With the information on the attitudes and 5 element types, we've been able to diagnose and adjust ourselves with surprising ease.

"Some problem areas, like production and shipping, have now become consistent and reliable. Productivity has soared, at all levels, with creativity at an all time high, and sales increasing at a 50% rate. The company feels more relaxed than ever, and has been able to clarify its future goals—all in only three months. This information cuts through to the most essential and practical needs of our business. From the most personal to the highly technical it provides the principles to make the correct decision or adjustment that is needed."
  —**Kevin Lindseth, Vice President, Long Life Products, Inc.**

"After having read *The Great Tao* and the Internal Exercises book, I came upon *The Integral Management of Tao*. At first I was surprised by the simplicity of the words and the simple direction that the sages recommended in this text. I thought, 'This can't work, it's just too simple.'

"Fortunately, I remembered that years ago I said the same thing about the Internal Exercises book, and I was proven completely wrong. Your exercises worked miracles for me. Because of this experience, I gave your book a serious try, reading it several times and studying the exercises in depth. Each time revealed new secrets of Power, Wealth, Joy and overall Balance in the management of my personal and financial life.

"I have taken many excellent training and self-empowering seminars including formal training at a graduate level in business and years of study of negotiation techniques. But no modern or ancient system I have come across harmonizes and synchronizes our physical, mental and spiritual bodies to aid us in our evolutionary mission as the philosophy you have laid out in the Integral Management and Great Tao books.

"Thanks to your work in translating, adapting and interpreting the works of Kue Ku Tzu and *Su Shu*, I have been able to create Sol y Luna International out of thin air. Any serious student will find in your works the depth and insight of Lao Tzu's *Tao Te Ching*, and the effectiveness of strategy and implementation of Sun Tzu's *Art of War* applied to personal and business management fields. Thank you for sharing your wisdom."

    —Fernando Moreno, Duke University MBA; Ex-Advisor, Minister of Finance, Ecuador; General Partner, Sol y Luna International

"Al and I have been reading your marvelous book *The Integral Management of Tao* aloud to each other and we are so impressed with the wisdom you are sharing with the world. Al is Vice President of Human Resources at Sunsweet so he is directly concerned with management techniques which will bring harmony and prosperity to all. We are looking forward to discussing these with you. Al has intuitively been using many of the techniques you advocate and wants to incorporate the rest of your advice as soon as possible. He has many stories about his personal experience to tell you. It is unusual for a man in Labor Relations to be promoted to Vice President and he attributes this honor to precisely the advice you are advocating."

    —Al and Barbara Vallejo

"I found that you have simplified a complex subject so beautifully that everyone from all walks of life could benefit from the knowledge put forth in the book.

"It was a realistic approach to a better life through proper and good management of time and effort to help one achieve one's goals in every area of one's life.

"It is a book to read and re-read and to keep near you as a reference book to aid you in the management of your life to constantly search for improvement."

    —Vera Brown, Author, President of Vera's Retreat Inc., Featured on *Life Styles of the Rich and Famous*, and Honored Woman of the Year by The City of Hope

"I found *The Integral Management of Tao* to be a most interesting and informative book. . . . I am with you in mind and spirit."

    —Phillip Schaeffer, President, Corporate Communications
    —Gita LaBrentz, Ph.D., Stanford University Professor

"Ideally, this book should be read by people prior to or at the beginning of their careers and during their whole work life, for its philosophies smoothe the everyday business of living into harmonious degrees of understanding.

"Universities might do well to consider adding *The Integral Management of Tao* to their required reading lists regardless of the course.

"This is a must book for all professions. I've enjoyed it!"
>—**Edvina Cahill, Chief Administrative Officer,**
>**San Francisco Unified School District**

"I have been doing the eye exercises. I had noticed that my right eye was blurry and seemed to have film over it. That condition has completely cleared."
>—**Kathryn Carlson, School Administrator and Teacher**

"For incurable patients, we need management medicine, which in my opinion, this book has contributed to a great deal."
>—**Thomas Schulte, M.D., Stanford University Medical**
>**School Professor**

Dissolve stress, tension, depression, fatigue and safeguard good health easily, safely, and effectively with Dr. Chang's stress management technique, preferred by top executives.
>—**As reported in *Fortune* magazine**

"The superfluous areas of the stomach and abdomen are literally rubbed away."
>—**Los Angeles Herald**

"Double happiness is so very important! We really enjoyed and learned from your management book the role of man and wife! You are in our thoughts and prayers always."
>—**Jana and Christopher O'Connor, Euro Bond Broker**

"Dr. Stephen T. Chang could have looked at David Stockman and Alexander Haig and told President Reagan that their associations with him were destined to fail. According to Taoist facial reading, their classifications clash."
>—**San Francisco Examiner**

"We live in a time of increasing specialization. It is rare to find anyone with the fine tuning of a microbiologist and the expansiveness of an astrophysicist. In this and in his earlier books however Dr. Chang is presenting us with a way of living in the world that is both ancient and modern, that functions on many levels, spiritual, global, interpersonal and self-actualizing.

". . . In *The Integral Management of Tao* we are given a method of organization, of how to function in the world. This material builds upon the personal work described in the earlier books. On the surface this seems to be a book for business people. The examples Dr. Chang gives us come from global corporations and from ancient empires. But if we think of ourselves as the CEO's of our private lives, then this book has much to say to all of us, in and out of the world of business.

"The two sections of this book are based upon timeless Taoist knowledge. At every step of the way we are shown the relationship between personal choices and the harmony of yin and yang in the cosmos. The movement of those two forces into eight directions, eight trigrams and eight exercises related to them supports a balanced individual making balanced choices. Then Dr. Chang explores the Chinese five element theory, shows how each element generates a basic personality type, and shows how an understanding of the relationships between those types can support an organization's smooth functioning, from a personal to the departmental level. Nothing, according to Dr. Chang, happens in isolation, and his philosophy offers a simple and useful model for understanding the connections between decisions, leaders, workers, products and the economy.

"The second section of the book is on the nature of leadership itself. It is about how to make right choices by understanding different styles of leadership and their consequences. Here we are shown how a knowledge of the five relations in Chinese thinking, parents, children, superior, subordinate and brother, can help to organize work decisions. There is information on different methods of communication and how each can be used with a different relation. There is also information on the nature of persuasion and how it can be best used in the business world. The appendix of the book brings all of this theoretical material back to the core again, the body, with exercises for vision and stress reduction, a side-effect of most work situations.

"While some knowledge of Dr. Chang's previous books can be helpful, this book can also stand on its own as a text in leadership training. It is practical and all-encompassing. As government and industry seem to be increasingly out of touch with both the planet and the people of the world, a book such as this seems to me both necessary and rare. If we are going to eliminate war, pollution, hunger and other world problems, we will need a global view such as Dr. Chang's. So this book is not just a self-help tool for individuals who want to improve their decision-making processes and their financial lives. It is also a guideline for rethinking the ways we have allowed government and industry to reshape, to un-shape our world. It's easy to become attached to what we want to do and what we want our governments to do. In *The Integral Management of Tao* Dr. Stephen Chang offers us a spiritual view of why and how we can improve our lives, from a personal to a global level."

—**Andrew Ramer, Author of** *Little Pictures: Fiction for a New Age* **and Co-author of** *The Spiritual Dimensions of Healing Addictions* **and** *Further Dimensions of Healing Addictions*

"*The Integral Managment of Tao* is a treasure of information bringing ancient and present knowledge of management into a contemporary synthesis. Reading I experienced myself on one side visiting the wise man who told me the secrets, rules and laws of the world; and on the other side I saw myself as an aspiring human being, manager, politician, getting familiar with the latest and finest in how to achieve. In a clear language the topics are organized and concentrated in compact statements, open to be applied for one's individual needs and they can again be expanded into endless possibilities of practical use. In a time of shortsightedness, greed, exploitation of the people and our planet one wishes for presidents, directors, managers with such a foundation in quality and integrity as described here. It is knowledge ready available for one's business and life to succeed. This clearly layed out concept of management confirms that a harmonious individual, company, society, and world could exist."

—**Judith Scherer, Internationally Known Choreographer**

". . . means a great deal to us and reminds us of the generous spirit of America."

—**James E. Carter, Author, Professor and Former President of the United States of America, and Mrs. Rosalynn Carter**

Ronald W. Reagan, Former President of the United States of America, honored Dr. Chang: "Stephen T. Chang has played a vital role in strengthening and safeguarding our nation's legacy of freedom, hope, prosperity and opportunity for all Americans." (1988)

A Discourse on Management
A Review on Dr. Stephen T. Chang's
The Integral Management of Tao: Complete Achievement
by Luke T. Chang, Ph.D.; President, Lincoln University

Some five years ago, through the medium of Mr. Thomas Yang, my friendship with Dr. Stephen T. Chang has developed ever since. Through his courtesy, I was able to enjoy reading his book on *The Great Tao*. It is a great work, so great that when I casually showed it to Mr. Robert Buckinmeyer of the California State Department of Education, he grabbed it. The book is an in-depth analysis of Chinese philosophy, particularly the Taoist sector. (The book was published by Tao Publishing, San Francisco 1985.)

Recently, Dr. Stephen Chang completed an equally remarkable work, *The Integral Management of Tao* (also published by Tao Publishing 1988). It is a theoretical approach of management based on Chinese history and philosophy, particularly from the teachings of the Yellow Emperor, Lao Tzu, Sage Kuei Ku Tzu and the Yellow Stone Sage. According to the author, Sage Kuei Ku's book, the *Kuei Ku Tzu,* was written in a rare form of archaic script; it took him special effort to master an ancient language—to read, study and decipher the book. The same is true for Dr. Chang on the Yellow Stone Sage's *Su Shu*. In addition, the *Kuei Ku Tzu* had been declared a forbidden work by feudal lords throughout the millennia, with no one in the ancient or modern world having access to it. I had only heard of *Kuei Ku Tzu,* never having an opportunity to obtain a copy of it.

I am in complete agreement with Dr. Chang when he asserts in his preface: "As long as human beings exist, management will exist. So long as people must live together, management will be needed."

The author divides *The Integral Management of Tao: Complete Achievement* into ten chapters:

1. The Tao of Evolution
2. The Tao of Yin and Yang Relativism
3. The Tao of Eight Attitudes
4. The Tao of Positioning
5. The Tao of Five-Star System
6. The Tao of Psycho-Dynamics
7. The Tao of Leadership
8. The Tao of Complete Resolution
9. The Tao of Intercommunication
10. The Tao of Riches and Fame

All the chapters are very penetrating in analyzing the subject matter, and are worth painstaking study and due diligent practice. But the chapter "The Tao of Five-Star System" was widely praised because he pointed out that "knowledge of personalities is of utmost importance in the working environment. If a manager assigns a 'wrong person' to work on a 'wrong job,' everything will go wrong" (p. 110).

In discussing the Five-Star System, which is really interpreting the Chinese philosophy of the <u>Yin-Yang</u> theory and the interplay of the Five Elements (Fire, Earth, Metal, Water and Wood), Dr. Chang pointed out a vivid example in using the system to determine the health of an organization. One of his associates counsels for a major U.S. investment bank interested in a South American country was sent there to examine the situation:

> In one week he diagnosed the problem and came up with all the corrective suggestions. Unfortunately, the bank did not appreciate his wonderful method and sent a group of so-called experts to the same location. It took them one year to learn what the problems exactly were. By the time their reports were completed the company in South America had already collapsed. The bank lost all its investments. Later the bank admitted that the diagnostic sections of the reports submitted by my associate and the experts were exactly the same. The only differences were that my associate's report included corrective solutions and was completed within a week and the experts' report offered no solution within a year. The bank spent a great fortune acquiring a great loss, just because it lacked this knowledge (p. 113).

Equally interesting was when Albert S. Humphrey, Chairman of Business Planning and Development in London, pointed out that he

> was part of a research team in 'management science' set up by Stanford Research Institute from 1965 through 1970. Our research resulted in statistically discovering the 3 factors which statistically separates successful companies and people from mediocrity.... I was disappointed to discover that these factors were already known in 1,200 BC and that Dr. Chang has written on this in Chapter V....[1]

This writer particularly admire chapter 8 on the decision-making process. The author elucidates the idea of three compositions from *Kuei Ku Tzu*. Each composition should explain one of three decisions to be chosen as the final decision by the decision-maker. Each decision must, therefore, be written out fully.

A composition must contain at least four paragraphs:

A. The first contains the theme (decision) and its exposition;
B. The second contains the major theory that supports the theme and the reasons, especially evidence, for the support;
C. The third contains opposing or differing points of view, and the reasons and evidence explaining why the decision may or may not be acceptable;
D. The fourth is the conclusion and explains why the chosen solution.

The sage suggests that a composition be four-sectioned, to assure completeness. Thus the formula incorporates both logical induction and deduction, in addition to eliciting dialectical demonstrations.

The book combines ancient wisdom with modern knowledge and high output techniques. After you finish reading it, you would feel you are a trained leader in your field with vision and ideas that work. You don't want to give up the book, as it is practical and all-encompassing for daily living and working.

Now, let me turn to my observation on management in the context of the global scene.

According to my observation, the vicissitudes of the corporations of various industries are mainly due to the quality of management. And the huge budget and trade deficit is also due to failure in governing. Management in private business and government for public interest are the same thing: both require good management.

Take the merchandise trade deficit as an example. Starting in the 1960's, the U.S. lost steadily its competitive advantage.[2] The chart at the end of this article shows that the U.S. position in world trade is shrinking.

The figures are based on U.S. Dept. of Commerce sources. It is widely known that U.S. merchandise lost its competitiveness because the U.S. government does not promote the Research and Development (R & D) as hard and effectively as the Japanese government (MITI) does. In addition, there are anti-trust laws which prevent private corporations from consolidating the resources to do the job. Herein the U.S. lost its competitiveness as well.

In addition, because there is no concentrated effort in R & D, the quality of U.S. goods is becoming less and less competitive with that of Japan and Germany, for example. Small wonder that one Japanese claimed that while in the U.S. he couldn't find anything made in the U.S. that could measure up to the "scrutiny of a quality-conscious Japanese." (There was only one perfect item: Vermont maple syrup.)[3]

However, credit should be given to the Bush Administration. It recently tried to improve the quality of products through the use of the "Malcom Baldridge National Quality Award." It entrusted the National Institute of Standards and Technology to be responsible for development and administering the awards. The first ones were awarded to Xerox Corporation's Business Products System and Milliken & Company.[4] How soon this kind of encouragement could have nation-wide effect remains to be seen, although President Bush on that occasion spoke of making painstaking reassessment and the drive to win back that market share.[5] Let me just pick another example: The Economic Policy Institute pointed out that the U.S. stands to lose two million jobs and suffer a $225 billion trade deficit by 2010 if the government fails to boost our industry to compete in high-definition television (HDTV), semi-conductors, computers and digital communication.[6]

As to the U.S. Budget deficit, the Federal Government is making efforts to reduce it, particularly through the Gramm-Rudman legislation. But bi-partisan Congressional Budget Office (CBO) recently estimated that continuing the status quo in spending and taxes would leave a budget deficit of about $135 billion in 1993.[7] To my mind, the following factors contributed to the persistent problem: (a) Social systems, particularly the SSI system. The original idea was good for helping the poor, but the result has been to discourage people from working, producing more homeless and drug users; (b) poor worker-training standards; (c) high consumption; and (d) a low savings rate.[8]

This is why a study shows that the Japanese gross product, on a per capita basis, will have grown at more than twice that of the U.S. by the year 2000. "Not only had the U.S. become a weak economy incapable of balancing its books, all it seemed able to do was blame Japan."[9]

More importantly, consider the fact that the U.S. is now the world's largest debtor, due to the mismanagement of the national budget deficit and international trade deficit. As Arthur Schlesinger puts it: "Total foreign claims on American assets have more than tripled during this careless decade."[10] He continues to point out its implications of national security if "Our creditors should register disapproval of government policies by dumping Treasury securities and other holdings on the market." It is indeed an iron law of history "that power passes from debtor to creditor" as Sen. Daniel Patrick Moynihan rightly declared.[11]

Finally, as the world political and economic scene changes, it is easy to blame the Japanese or Germans. Yes, Germany and Japan do pose problems for the U.S. in the future. But "German-bashing or Japan-bashing is a formula for escaping our difficulties, not for solving them," as Schlesinger correctly concludes in his article. "Our problem is not Japan or Germany."[12]

Therefore, how are we going to solve the problem for the U.S.?

I believe that the basic approach to the solution of the previous discussed issues is education, but not just because I am an educator.

In general, American workers need better schooling and more job training in comparison with their German or Japanese counterparts. They must learn to capture emerging high-technology markets with the greatest opportunity for growth and profit, as the Japanese have done in the past. There is no doubt that Japanese schools produce less dissenting students, who usually receive better discipline; one does not hear much of dropouts or drug addicts. One also does not know of schools producing a glut of lawyers who lead to a glut of litigation in which the law itself does not become a settled or predictable framework for justice.

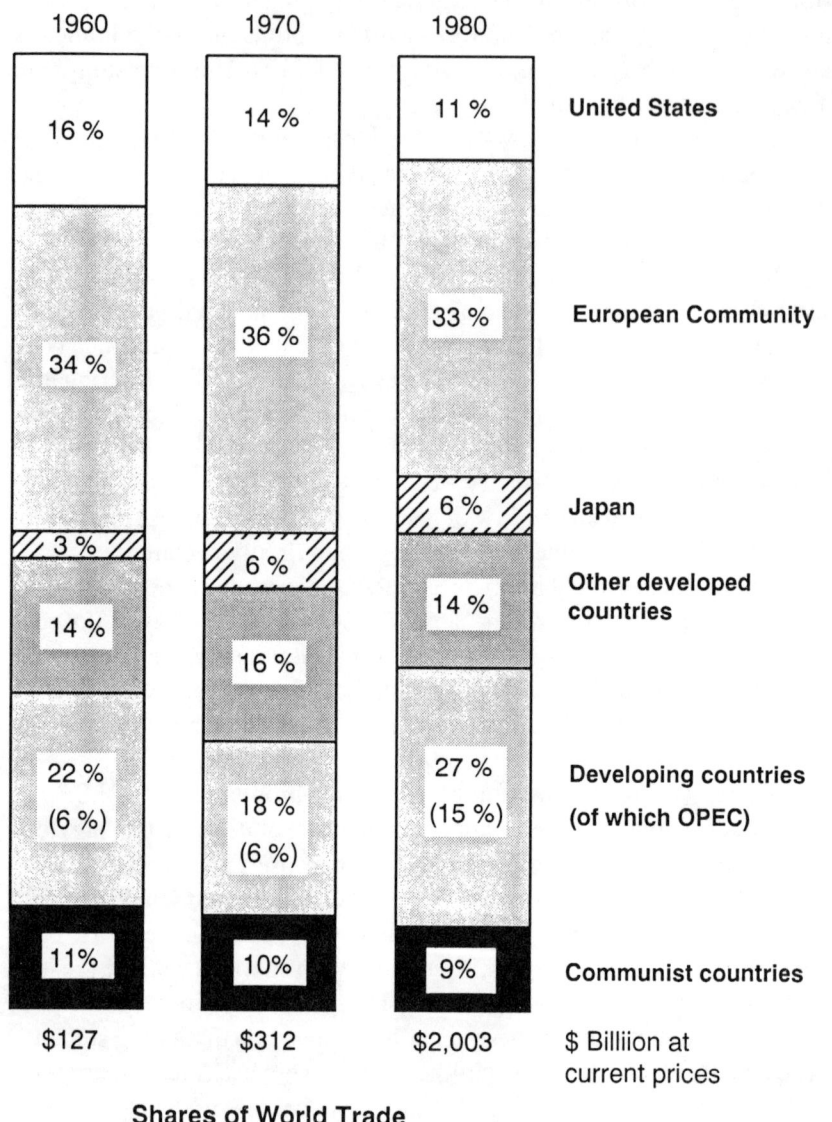

Perhaps these are the reasons why when Mr. George Bush was a candidate for President, he called for a "Coalition of Education America" in July 1988 and declared himself the "Education President."[13]

Lately, as President of the United States, he conferred with the Governors at the Governors Confab (?), brought out his campaign proposal of $500 million in federal aid to encourage improvement in elementary and secondary school education as well as in research projects.

Whatever President Bush and his administration might do for American education or economy, I would like to emphasize what I have said before: "The current activist advocates 'Human Rights.' We at Lincoln Univeristy lecture on human values. We believe that through proper education, the young people can be improved in their intellectual and ethical standards, thus enhancing human values and maximize the shareholder value of corporations."[14]

Above all, modern management covers so many fields and specialties. But fundamentally, one needs to start with ancient wisdom encompassed in *The Integral Management of Tao*.

NOTES

1. Quoted from a brochure compiling past book reviews of Dr. Chang's work which was also published by Tao Publishing.
2. Reprinted from Raymond J. Waldmann, *Managed Trade, The New Competition Between Nations*, Ballinger Publishing Co., Cambridge, Massachusetts: 1986.
3. Quoted from *Best of Business*, Spring 1989, p. 56.
4. Refer to *Business America*, November 20, 1989: pp. 2-11.
5. Quoted from *Business America*, November 20, 1989: pp. 2-15.
6. *San Francisco Examiner*, November 20, 1989 B3.
7. *The Wall Street Journal*, May 25, 1989: A27.
8. Organization for Economic Corporation and Development. (See chart)
9. *Best of Business*, Spring 1989: 56.
10. *The Wall Street Journal*, December 22, 1989: A6.
11. Ibid.
12. Ibid.

U.S. Saving Rate Lags in '80s
Private and government saving percentage of gross domestic product, 1980-87

Japan	31.1%
Germany	21.8%
Canada	19.9%
Italy	19.6%
France	19.3%
Britain	18.0%
U.S.	16.9%

Source: Organization for Economic Cooperation and Development

13. This writer was asked to participate in the Coalition of Education meeting in Washington, D.C., in July 1988.
14. Quoted from the writer's unpublished speech delivered at the 1989 Commencement of Lincoln University in San Francisco.

In addition, President Bush in his recent annual budget message revealed comparisons of savings rates of the world industrial powers. This writer reproduces them in the following for the reader's reference.

How Savings Rates Compare
Net saving as a percentage of net national income; averages 1980-87

	TOTAL	GOVERNMENT*	HOUSEHOLDS	ENTERPRISES
Japan	20.3%	4.1%	13.5%	2.7%
Italy	12.8	N.A	N.A	N.A
Germany	10.8	1.4	8.9	0.5
Canada	9.9	-3.9	9.7	4.1
France	8.6	N.A	N.A	N.A
U.K.	6.3	-1.6	5.0	3.4
United States	4.2	-3.9	6.2	2.0
U.S. ranking	7/7	4/5	4/5	4/5

*Includes some public physical capital investment as saving   N.A=Not available
Source: Office of Management and Budget